The Final Hour Unveiled

10 Prophetic Revelations Before Judgment Day

Nada Adams

Searaj Ad-Dean Publishing

Credit: Image Art sketches by Mariam Chamy visit Instagram store: @art_bymariam

Sacred Veil . com

Contents

Introduction

Praise be to the Lord of the universe; to God belongs all the creations. May Allah elevate Prophet Muhammad, peace be upon him, his family, and Companions, and protect his nation from harm.

With the world in decline, it's crucial to spread the spiritual truth about prophecies that signal the approach of Judgment Day. The present state of the world is one of uncertainty, fear, and desperation. Widespread panic over the last few years, with people living in constant fear, only compounds the anxiety and despair many feel.

It's natural to seek help from any available sources in times like these. However, societies must recognize that God is the only one who provides proper protection and guidance. Only through our belief in God and our reliance on Him can we find peace and comfort in turbulent times.

In the Quran, God reveals that He is the protects believers in **Surah Al-Baqarah, verse 257**, which means,

> **<<Allah is the Supporter/Protector of those who believe. He brings them out of darkness into the light (of truth). And those who disbelieve their allies are false gods who take them out of the light (of truth) and into darkness (of disbelief, doubt, and sins). Those are the companions of the Fire where they will abide forever therein.>>**

This verse reminds humanity that it is only through our belief in God that we can find our way out of the darkness and into the light.

The Quran contains many prophecies that have come true and continue to come true to this day. These prophecies serve as a reminder of God's power and control over the universe, guidance to navigate life's challenges, and signs of Islam's truth and validity.

One such prophecy is the Quran's Prophet Joseph story. Joseph's brothers sold him into slavery, and someone else accused him of a crime he did not commit, resulting in his wrongful imprisonment. However, Joseph, peace be upon him, overcame these challenges through his unwavering faith in God and eventually became the King of Egypt.

Another prophecy in the Quran is the story of Prophet Muhammad: peace be upon him. The Quran contains many verses that convey the honorable life of Prophet Muhammad, his teachings, and his mission that continue to guide millions of Muslims worldwide today.

Prophet Muhammad's life shows the power of faith and relying on God, especially in tough times. Despite facing many challenges and opposition throughout his honorable life, Prophet Muhammad, peace be upon him, remained steadfast in his belief in God and the spread of Islam.

> *This story reminds us that no matter how difficult our circumstances become, we must never lose faith in God, who if God wills, will turn our hardships into blessings and transform our world into a better future.*

As we continue to navigate the challenges of this life, it is essential to remember that our time on this Earth is finite. The prophecies in the Quran warn that the Day of Resurrection is drawing closer and closer.

Judgment Day is a day of great horror for most people and jinn because they died as disbelievers. Everyone will witness their evil deeds exposed and on display.

In the Quran, God reveals that on this day, there will be no escape from the consequences of our actions.

> In **Surah Al-Baqarah, verse 281,** means, **<<Fear the Day when you will be brought back <for**

> **Judgment>. Allah will give each soul its due reward on that day, and there will be no injustice.>>**

The prophecies emphasize the significance of following God and leading a righteous life to humanity. The sane and conscious person must constantly strive to do good deeds, avoid sins, and seek forgiveness from God for their mistakes. Those who adhere to these principles can legitimately hope to be among the fortunate who receive God's mercy on the Day of Resurrection.

> God revealed in the Quran in **Surah Al-Qiyamah, verses 1-2** mean, **<<I <God> swear by the Day of Resurrection. And I <God> swear by the self-reproaching soul (to the certainty of resurrection).>>**

These prophecies, warning humanity for over 1500 years, must not be taken lightly.

- Our purpose and why we're on this Earth is to believe in Allah and His Messengers – the original and authentic creed.
- Adhere to our religious duties and refrain from sins as ordained by God.
- To ask God for forgiveness.

- To be conscious that each day on Earth could be our last, so we must live every day being steadfast to Islam until death.

Accumulating wealth at the expense of others' well-being does not equate to a fulfilling life. The elites' lives are often rooted in disregarding God's commands and building their wealth empires through sinful means.

Contrary to popular belief, the extremely intelligent are only sometimes the wealthiest. The smart people are the believers who train themselves daily to perform more good deeds than they accomplished the day before. They know that accumulating wealth on Earth won't guarantee entry into Paradise, so they're willing to prioritize piety over financial gain.

The prophecies are factual events that God has predestined to exist in the future. Seekers of Paradise will take heed and remain steadfast to a life of righteousness for a blissful outcome.

The Day of Judgment will be a very long and frightening day filled with horror for most humanity and jinn to witness. However, blissful mercy awaits only those who obey God in this earthly life.

We must always remember our religious priorities as we navigate the challenges of our declining world. These prophecies warn and remind humanity, those who are conscious, that Judgment Day is drawing closer and closer.

God revealed in the Holy Qur'an in **Surat Muhammad Verse 18** means, <<**Do they await only the Hour that it comes to them suddenly? For indeed, its signs have already arrived! Then, how can they have their reminder when the Hour comes to them?**>>

Allah, the Creator of the universe, created life on Earth as a temporary pathway to the Hereafter, not a permanent home. Our fleeting life should not discourage but motivate us to make the most of our time by acquiring good deeds diligently, seeking forgiveness for our mistakes, and preparing ourselves for the Hereafter.

Our ultimate purpose in this earthly life is to worship Allah alone, seeking His Acceptance. The prophecies of the Hereafter serve to warn and remind humanity of the importance of preparing for our final destination.

No one is God except Allah.
No one is a Creator other than Allah.

Our ultimate purpose in this earthly life is to worship Allah alone seeking His Acceptance. The prophecies of the Hereafter serve to warn and remind humanity of the importance of preparing for our final destination.

God revealed in **Surat Ghafir, Verse 59** means, **<<The Hour will certainly come. There is no doubt—Yet most men believe not.>>**

> God revealed in **Surah Al-Anbiya, verse 35,** means, **<<Every soul shall taste death. And We test you <O humanity> with evil and with good as trial; and to Allah you shall be returned <for judgment>.>>**

This verse reminds us that death is inevitable and that we will all be tested by good and evil in this life. It is up to us to choose how we respond to these tests and live our lives. The Quran also tells us that the purpose of our existence on this Earth is to worship Allah alone.

> God revealed in **Surah Adh-Dhariyat, verse 56** means, **<<And I did not create the Jinn and Humans except <to be ordered> to worship <God>.>>**

This verse explicitly states our purpose in this earthly life: to worship Allah and seek His Acceptance. The Quran tells us that the Hereafter is a place of everlasting happiness or everlasting punishment, depending on how we live on this Earth.

> God revealed in **Surah Al-Ma^arij, verses 15-16** which means, **<<Indeed, it is the flame <of Hellfire>. A remover of exteriors <the severity of Hellfire flays skin>.>>**

These verses explicitly describe one aspect of the punishment in the Hereafter for those who choose blasphemy over faith and die as accountable blasphemers.

All that exists on this Earth is transient and will eventually die and end, taking all life on Earth as we know it. Nothing on this Earth is permanent. Even the grandeur of the mountains, once towering above the fragility of humankind, will crumble into insignificant specks of dust.

Since the dawn of human existence, people are born and die daily. This cycle will continue until everything and everyone on Earth, including humans, jinn, and animals, will meet their earthly demise.

The inevitability of death looms over every living being, and no one can escape God's decree.

Even the angels, including the revered Angel Israfeel who blows the horn, and the Honorable Angel of Death, Azra'eel, who takes the souls of all living beings on Earth, God will create death for the Angel of Death, signifying the end of all life on Earth.

The companions were sitting together, speaking about the day of judgment. Prophet Muhammad, peace be upon him, was seated in an elevated area and looked over at the companions asking them about their discussion.

> The Prophet, peace be upon him, said, **"You will not see Judgment Day until 10 (major) signs appear."**

These signs serve as a severe warning to humanity, urging them to repent and become believers before it is too late. The appearance of these signs one after the other is a reminder that the Day of Resurrection is nearing and that every person should prepare themselves for that day by living a righteous life and seeking Allah's guidance and forgiveness.

CHAPTER 1

THEY ASK YOU ABOUT THE FINAL HOUR...

ALTHOUGH THE EXACT DATE and time of the world's end are unknown, the Prophet, peace be upon him, conveyed minor and major signs that will serve as a warning that Judgment Day is drawing nearer.

God concealed the exact time of Judgment Day from everyone, including the angels, as made apparent when Angel Gabriel visited the Prophet and his companions.

He asked the Prophet several questions to expand the knowledge of Islam among his companions.

The Quran emphasizes that nothing in this life is permanent, and everything on Earth will eventually perish and die one day, as nothing in this life will last forever.

When?

The precise time and date are unknown to all creations, as confirmed in the Qur'an that Allah the Exalted has concealed the exact time of Judgment Day from even the highest-ranking angels and the best of creations, all the Prophets and Messengers.

> Allah revealed in Chapter Al-Aˆraf, Verse 187 that means << **“They ask you** <O Muhammad> **about the final hour, when's the appointed time? Say the knowledge of it is known only by my Lord. None, but He knows when it will be.** <Its knowledge> **is weighty upon the inhabitants of the heavens and earth. It will not come to you except suddenly.”** >>

Imam Muslim related that Angel Gabriel once appeared to the Prophet in the apparent form of a young man (without genitals) and sat among his companions.

One question Angel Gabriel asked was, **“Tell me about the Day of Judgment?”**

The Prophet replied, **“I know no more about it than you do.”**

By this, the Prophet meant both Angel Gabriel and he knew nothing about the destined time of the Day of Judgment.

Angel Gabriel requested, **“Then tell me about the Signs of the Day of Judgment?”**

The Prophet, peace be upon him, replied, **“The Day of Judgment will arrive after the girls harm their mothers immensely. They treat their mothers like their slaves, and the peasants with the shepherds who were both barefoot and poor, will be wealthy enough to build tall buildings.”**

> In the Hadith the Prophet, peace be upon him, said, "**Hurry to do <good> deeds before trial and tribulations of the night overwhelm you. Where a person will awaken a believer but become a disbeliever by night or be a believer at night and awaken a nonbeliever. Where people will sell their faith (Islam) for worldly possessions that are worthless and hold little value.**"

> The Prophet, peace be upon him, said, "**A time will come upon people wherein the one steadfast to their religion <Islam> will be like those holding burning coals.**"

Allah has revealed the *'Minor and Major Signs'* that will indicate the Approach of the Day of Resurrection.

The minor signs, which have been occurring slowly since the time of Prophet Muhammad over 1497 years ago, must all appear first and continue happening for a long time. After that, the first of the Major Signs will appear.

As the time draws closer to Judgment Day, all the Minor Signs will finish appearing, and the Major Signs will begin.

The Major Signs will occur more rapidly in a relatively shorter period once the first Major Sign appears.

In the finale, life on Earth will suddenly end with a sudden blow.

Chapter 2

Awaiting The Last Minor Sign

Prophet Muhamad conveyed the signs that mark the **'Last Hour'** as approaching and drawing nearer.

Islam categorizes these signs—as Minor and Major Signs.

Some signs will appear before the Day of Judgment, cited in the Qur'an and the Prophetic Hadith.

Many minor signs will appear first, and the ten major signs begin afterward.

Imam Muslim narrated in his book "As-Sahih" from the Companion Hudhayfah Ibn-ul-Yaman and others that when Prophet Muhammad, peace be upon him, was in a session with some of his Companions, he conveyed some of the events that would occur before the Day of Judgment.

One of the Minor Signs mentioned by the Prophet is **"Widespread killing of innocent people by killers with no motive or valid reason."**

The Prophet (peace be upon him) mentioned a Hadith that praises those who remain steadfast in fulfilling their obligations during difficult times.

> **"During a period of widespread unjust killing on Earth, a believer who performs their obligations and acts of worship would receive a reward similar to that of the Muslim companions who migrated to the Prophet during a time when migration was an obligation on Muslims, before the opening of Makkah."**
>
> Our Prophet said, **"Some of my nation shall always stay steadfast to the truth in an apparent way, and no one can harm their call until Judgment Day."**

The Prophet did not say, "until the last moment before the Day of Judgment." Hence, as long as the Nation of Prophet Muhammad exists, there will always be people from his community who remain steadfast to the truth. No one has the power to cancel their call.

Before the last 100 years on Earth, God will make all the Muslims die so that only blasphemers remain alive. For an entire century, there will be no person on Earth who worships or praises God, only evil idol worshipers.

One day, suddenly, when these evil people least expect it, the angel will blow the horn, killing every creation alive. Afterward, the Day of Judgment will begin at its designated time.

Most of the Minor Signs have happened. However, the remarkable Major Signs begin once the final minor sign arrives.

Some Minor Signs:

- Some whole mountains will be removed (disappear) from their bases
- Some people will claim to be <false> prophets at least 30+
- Increase of Earthquake occurrences
- A population of deceivers and misleaders—among them will be the preachers of corruption
- Diseases unfamiliar to society will spread
- Fornication and adultery will be widespread
- Consumption of Wine (alcohol) is excessive
- People will compete to make tall buildings
- Significant positions will be filled with unqualified people

- Detectable changes to the weather
- Widespread events of killings and injustice will occur
- Close distances between shopping centers
- It is rare to find a person who prays with genuine humbleness and humility in a mosque.
- There will be a speedy lapse of time, whereby a year would pass by like a month, a month would pass by like a week, and a week would feel like one day.

Other nations will take advantage of the Muslim nation's fortunes. Similar to the person who takes advantage of a delicious banquet of food while being surrounded from all directions. (The current reality in the Middle East)

Another minor sign of the Day of Judgment cited by the Prophet is the Euphrates River will change its course, and a sizeable amount of gold will appear. As a result, people will fight viciously to capture the gold within, leading to the death of 99% of those who fight for it. The Prophet warned the Muslims not to pursue getting this gold.

Imam Muslim narrated that the Prophet said, **"Islam started strange among the people (who worshiped idols). And, it will return to be strange <to the people> like the way it began <to the Arabs>." This is due to the massive ignorance from the true teachings of Authentic Islam.**

That is our world's reality today. Adhering to the rules of the

Religion will bring difficulty, as stated by the Prophet, peace be upon him.

Imam Muslim reported a narration from the Prophet stating that the minor signs include immense hardships for the believers. Calamities will be so intense upon the believers that they will prefer to be dead and buried upon seeing the grave of their Muslim brother.

All these minor indications, events, and signs mentioned have occurred and will continue to occur. The minor signs have been happening for a long time and will continue until the occurrence of the first major sign.

Unlike the minor signs that have been occurring for nearly 15 centuries, the major signs, once they appear, will rapidly occur in comparison one after another in a much shorter period.

The Appearance of The Guided One: Master Al-Mahdiyy

Among the minor signs is the appearance of Al-Mahdiyy (The Guided), Muhammad, the son of ^Abdullah. He is a pious, just person from the lineage of the Prophet who will enforce the rules of Islam. The long-awaited last minor sign is yet to happen.

The Righteous Waliyy, Al-Mahdiyy's, is the last Minor sign, and he is already alive and will appear for rulership soon,

God Willing. As our crumbling political world increases in injustice, oppression, murder, and tyrannical agendas, the only remedy for humanity will be this Great Honorable Master Leader.

When the prophecy of this blessed man appears, he will bring a much-needed end to this new world order and the criminals behind it.

The elites, who feel more entitled than the impoverished, are no different from ancient Pharaohs who declared themselves gods and committed so much evil. God will terminate them and their evil agenda one day because nothing lasts forever here on Earth. Every empire has a rise and fall

Who is this blessed man? Master Al-Mahdiyy.

The Shiites claim that Al-Mahdiyy was their twelfth imam, who disappeared centuries ago, and that he was still alive in a dungeon and would one day reappear and rescue the world from this state of severe cruelty and injustice, filling it with justice.

But, the People of Truth, who are The True Followers of Prophet Muhammad called **Ahlu-s-Sunnah,** say, **'Al-Mahdiyy has not come yet'** because Prophet Muhammad, peace be upon him, said that he will appear near the end of times.

"The Day of Judgment will only occur after a man from my descendants will reign. His name is the same as mine, and his father's name is the same as my father's name. He will spread justice and fairness on Earth, after it was congested with injustice and oppression prior to his appearance."

"Imam Al-Mahdiyy will appear at the end of times when injustice has encompassed the entire Earth. His name will be Muhammad, the son of ^Abdullah, from Imam Al-Hassan or Al-Hussein (The sons of Lady Fatimah)."

Related by Ibn-Hibban in his book as-Sahih, Abu Dawud in his book as-Sunnan and At-Tirmidhiyy in his book al-Jami^ and Al-Hakim in his book called Al-Mustadrak, as related from the companion ^Abdullah Ibn Mas^ud, may Allah raise his rank, as he heard it from the Prophet, peace be upon him.

Prophet Muhammad, peace be upon him, said, **'An angel will go with him announcing, "O people, this is the Khalifah of Allah Al-Mahdiyy, follow him'."**

From the route of the Companions, that Prophet Muhammad, peace be upon him, said,

> **"When Al-Mahdiyy appears, he will come out from Madinah accompanied by three thousand angels. Three hundred and thirteen from the Awliya' (upright, pious Muslim Sufis) will await him in Makkah; they are the first ones to pledge allegiance to him. A large army from the Levant (Ash-Sham) countries will attack and fight Al-Mahdiyy. Allah will create a fissure earthquake on their path that will cave onto the entire military, swallowing them. After that incident, Al-Mahdiyy travels to the land of ash-Sham (Levant region), rules with justice, and takes over the Aqsa Mosque in Jerusalem. A famine will occur during the days of Al-Mahdiyy, and the pious believer will be satiated by doing Dhikr."**

Al-Mahdiyy is alive today, already the highest religious scholar and best Sufi of our time, but God has not ordered him to the Caliph yet.

DHIKR ARE STATEMENTS THAT **Glorify and Exalt the Creator.** Here are some Examples:

1. ***Laa ilaaha illal-Allah*** (No one is God but Allah is the best dhikr) ~ Say 1000 times daily

2. ***SubhanAllaah*** (God does not resemble the creations) ~ Say 100 times daily

3. ***Alhamdulillaah*** (Praise and glory and thanks be to God) – Say 100 times daily

4. ***Allaah Akbar*** (God is the greatest in Rank) – Say 100 times daily

5. ***Laa Hawlaa walaa Quwwata illa-billah*** (No one can evade sins or have strength to obey without God creating it) ~ Say often...100-300 daily

6. ***Hasbiya Allah wa niˆmal wakeel*** (My Lord's aid suffices me) ~ Say 300 times daily and many more.

Chapter 3

Major Sign No. 1

The Emergence of the (Antichrist) Ad-Dajjal

Who is the One-Eyed Imposter?

He is a human from the Children of Adam, apparently, from the Children of Isra'eel—a descendant from the children of Prophet Jacob, peace be upon all the Prophets.

> Prophet Muhammad, peace be upon him, described him as a terrible deceiver and liar—with one eye protruding resembling a bulging grape, while the other one as a flat, blind eye. His body is huge and tall, and his hair resembles the branches of trees. He is a vile but powerful man.

The Emergence of Ad-Dajjal is the First Major Sign of the approach of the Day of Judgment.

He is called **"Al-Masih ad-Dajjal"** which means **"One-Eyed Deceiver,"** because he is a blasphemer who sweeps through the land with tremendous and unusual speed.

Also called, **"Al-Masih Al-Kadhab"** which means **"One-Eyed Imposter and Liar."**

In confinement and chained by angels on an unknown island, this powerful man met one of the companions of Prophet Muhammad, peace be upon him.

What is Al-Jassassa?

Tamim Ibn Aws and his companions were lost at sea for a month before drifting onto an island. As soon as they stepped onto the island, a strange animal greeted them covered with so much hair—they could not distinguish its front from its back and spoke to them in the native tongue of Arabic. It frightened the Companions as they thought it was a devil.

This animal, named 'Jassassa,' told the newcomers on the island, **"Go to this man. He is most excited to hear your news."** Upon arrival, they found a large man chained up from the neck downward.

When he saw them, he began asking them questions, **"Inform me about the illiterate Prophet. What has he done?"**—meaning Prophet Muhammad, peace be upon him.

He knows his release will only be after the revelation of Prophethood to Muhammad, peace be upon him, and he wants to measure the remaining term of his imprisonment because he knows his release will be the first of the Major signs indicating the nearing of the Day of Judgment.

Tamim, the companion, replied, **"He (Prophet Muhammad) appeared and left Mecca and immigrated to Yathrib (The City of Medina)."**

The chained man seemed to know that event, so he asked, **"Did the Arabs fight him?"** Tamim replied, **"Yes."**

The imprisoned man asked, **"What did he (Prophet Muhammad) do with them?"** Tamim answered, **"He appeared to the Arabs (as a Prophet), and some of the Arabs believed in him and obeyed him,** i.e., became Muslims."

The confined man declared, **"It is better for them they obey him (Prophet Muhammad). Now, let me tell you about who I am. I am the Massih Ad-Dajjal, and my release will be soon."**

God revealed the description of the Imposter to Prophet Muhammad, peace be upon him, and which corresponded with the story of the companion Tamim. Ad-Dajjal will have extraordinary powers given to him by Allah, the Exalted.

Signs Before His Release...

> The Holy Prophet, peace be upon him, said, **"This is Taybah (Medina), this is Taybah, this is Taybah."** and **"The terror of the Imposter Ad-Dajjal will not enter Madinah. On that day, there will be 7 doors with armed Angels."**

The day Ad-Dajjal is released begins the first of the Major Signs, and what a calamity that will be for the entire world! He will gain access to every place and village on Earth except entry into Makkah and Medina in Saudi Arabia because, at every gateway, an angel is guarding the entrance with his sword drawn, making Dajjal flee at their sight. God will ease ad-Dajjal's travels, so he travels strangely, unlike ordinary humans, and leads most of the world's population astray, causing people to fall into blasphemy almost everywhere he goes.

God will give a notable sign 3 years before his appearance and release:

- **Three years before** the arrival of Ad-Dajjal, the sky will hold one-third of its water.
- **Two years before,** the sky will reduce two-thirds of its water; and
- **One year before** his appearance, the sky will retain all its moisture—the entire world will experience one of the worst droughts, hunger, struggle, and famine.

Upon his emergence, how will the believer become satiated?

God will replace the need for sustenance and food for the believer without causing them physical harm. So, the Muslim will praise Allah, the exalted with Dhikr words, and by these honorable words, God creates for them nourishment and satiation.

The Dajjal imposter will travel the entire world in a rapid, strange manner, with tremendous ease given to him by God, unlike our ways of travel. Spreading corruption and blasphemy everywhere he goes, Dajjal travels the entire Earth from every direction in approximately one year and two and a half months. God will spare no village from his terror except two blessed cities—Makkah and Medina, Saudi Arabia.

How Long will The Anti-Christ/ Ad-Dajjal Roam the Earth?

> Prophet Mu_h_ammad peace be upon him conveyed, **"When the Imposter first appears to the world, He will roam the earth for forty days—his first day will feel as long as a year, the second day will feel as long as a month, the third day as long as a week and the remaining 37 days like your days."**

Allah will create great ease for this evil man to circumnavigate the globe in about one year and 70 days. At first, he will claim to be a Prophet and then arrogantly claim Godhood. His appearance will lead to widespread global blasphemy.

Currently, angels are restraining him with chains on an island until his due time, and his whereabouts remain unknown.

Ad-Dajjal will have extraordinary powers—given to him by Allah, the Exalted.

Excessive evil, seduction, and transgression will occur. Dajjal tells the sky to rain, and God creates the rain. Dajjal will tell the ground to grow its fruits, and God creates the land to produce them. Dajjal's evil commands occur because God creates the fulfillment of his commands, not because Dajjal is good or on the true spiritual path. But God created Dajjal as the biggest lure and deceiver in the history of humanity.

Ad-Dajjal is the worst human blasphemer ever to exist, arrogantly lying and claiming Godhood—that will result in misguiding and deceiving billions of people worldwide. Sadly, he will deceive most of the world's population and is destined for Hellfire in the Hereafter with all his followers.

O Allah. Protect us from his evil lures and transgressions.
Allahumma Ameen!

The extraordinary events that occur by Ad-Dajjal's command are not Miracles because he is a blasphemer and not a Prophet. Instead, these events are called in Arabic **"Istidraaj," which** means **'A LURE for the Misguided to increase in Misguidance.'**

His '**Lure**' is a vast calamity created by God for all His Slaves on Earth, as it will be **humanity's biggest test of faith.** This enormous lure exposes who among the people will stay steadfast to Islam and who will abandon their faith in God for the desire for comfort. Most people will sell their faith for the lure of the temporary, fleeting comfort of this world.

God will reveal who are the patient Muslims that stay steadfast to Islam and dedicated to worshipping God alone while exposing that most people are weak and will abandon their faith for fleeting worldly pleasures.

Satan is the absolute worst blasphemer, and Ad-Dajjal is the evilest Human Blasphemer. God sends Ad-Dajjal as a test to expose humanity's weaknesses and willingness to choose blasphemy over faith and lose the Afterlife forever.

Dajjal will deceive most people on Earth in various ways. He will claim to be a Prophet initially, and afterward, he will declare to be a deity. May Allah protect us from such evil.

He will speak blasphemy everywhere he goes, saying, **"I am your Lord, Most High (status)."**

Prophet Muhammad informed that many Jewish people will worship Dajjal, becoming his followers because they will follow the wealth. All people worldwide whom God willed to die blasphemers will follow this evil man. In Palestine, Dajjal's followers will be 70,000 Jews at that time.

Hunger and famine will cover the Earth for all people who choose to stay Muslims; since famine will not affect the blasphemers who follow and worship Dajjal—they will consider following Dajjal a blessing when, in fact, it's a curse.

God gives blasphemers temporary pleasure—they will have plenty of food and alleged good fortune. But the Muslims who reject the Imposter and stay steadfast to Islam will experience hunger pains only relieved through Dhikr—mentioning words that Glorify God.

God will provide the believers' protection from malnutrition by speaking these blessed words in place of food.

The Prophet, peace be upon him, said,

"Among the extraordinary things Ad-Dajjal displays—by God's will—is splitting a person in half, then restoring him together by God's will and creating. Ad-Dajjal will pass by arid land and order it to extract its treasures, and it will do so. These treasures will surface and follow Al-Dajjal like a swarm of bees."

Imagine the greedy leaders of today's corporations staring at that!

Prophet Muhammad, peace be upon him, conveyed the following story regarding a very courageous Muslim man who will be of a high rank from this nation who will approach Ad-Dajjal and tell him, **"I testify that you**

are the imposter that the Messenger of God (Muhammad) informed us."

Dajjal will ask his companions, ***"If I kill this man and bring him back to life, will you doubt my status?"***

They will reply, **'No.'** The Imposter Dajjal kills this Muslim man by cutting him in vertical halves and then returns him to life—by God creating everything.

O Allah, how much Ad-Dajjal will be a massive calamity and evil lure for the people?

When this Muslim man returns to life, he tells Dajjal, **"<Wallahi> By Allah, today I am most certain about what I know, that you are the Imposter Ad-Dajjal."**

Wanting to kill this man permanently, Ad-Dajjal cannot because God has willed for Master Al-Khadir to live the longest.

WHO IS THIS HIGH-RANKING MAN THAT DAJJAL CANNOT KILL?

Imam Muslim said, ***"He is Prophet Al-Khadir, peace be upon him***, "his full story of 'How and Why' God granted this honorable Prophet the longest human life on Earth in ***"Chapter 7—The Longest Living Human"***.

Examples of Ad-Dajjal's Powers...

Ad-Dajjal will have with him as he travels two flowing rivers—one river of fire and one river of water.

> Prophet Muhammad said in warning what means,
>
> **"As an added test, Ad-Dajjal will bring two rivers. One will seem to be fire, and the other will appear to be water. (Prophet Muhammad, peace be upon him, urges the Muslims to) rush themselves into the river that seems to be fire because, in reality, it's of the purest water. The believers will drink from it and walk out safely. But the river that appears to be water will be of fire."**

What will the Muslims do?

The Muslim male or female will close their eyes and walk towards the river of fire, which, in reality—will be safe for them. Among the Dajjal's severe transgressions, he will come to a Bedouin (Ârabiy) and say to him, *"If I resurrect your mother and father, will you testify I am your lord?"*

The Bedouin replies, "Yes." (The Bedouin blasphemed by saying this one word, i.e., 'Yes' to that evil question)

Two devils will appear in the image of his parents, and they will say to him, *"O son, follow him—he is your lord."*

Allahu Akbar how tragic!! Devils will appear as this Bedouin's parents and tell him to commit blasphemy! May Allah protect us from his transgressions and temptations. Ameen!

Chapter 4

How To Protect Yourself From Dajjal?

Prophet Muhammad, peace be upon him, warned us not to be impressed by the lure and events of Ad-Dajjal. Our Honorable Prophet urged us to stay firm in our belief in Allah, the Exalted, which will shield us from the fatal influence of the Major Deceiver, the likes of which no human on Earth has ever seen such intensity.

Prophet Jesus, peace be upon him, will kill this wicked, evil man at the gate of Ludd—a small village in Palestine.

> Prophet Muhammad, peace be upon him, said what means, **"Whoever memorizes 10 Ayat from the beginning of Surat Al-Kahf, God will protect him from Dajjal."**

These ten verses have proper interpretations, not direct translations, as Arabic is too eloquent to be translated into simple English words.

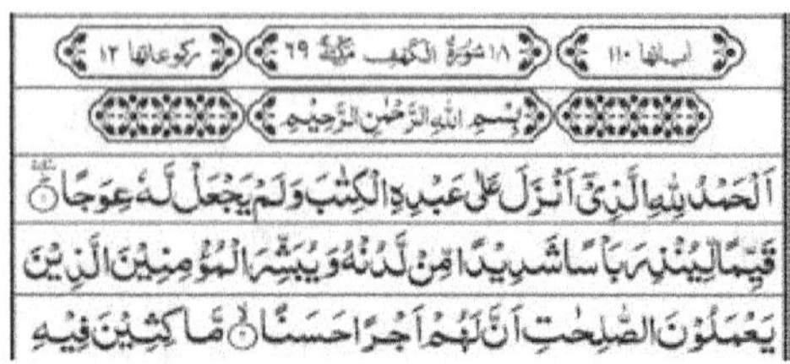

اٰياتها ١١٠ — ١٨ سُوْرَةُ الْكَهْفِ مَكِّيَّةٌ ٦٩ — رُكُوعَاتُهَا ١٢

بِسْمِ اللّٰهِ الرَّحْمٰنِ الرَّحِيْمِ

اَلْحَمْدُ لِلّٰهِ الَّذِيْٓ اَنْزَلَ عَلٰى عَبْدِهِ الْكِتٰبَ وَلَمْ يَجْعَلْ لَّهٗ عِوَجًا ۞
قَيِّمًا لِّيُنْذِرَ بَاْسًا شَدِيْدًا مِّنْ لَّدُنْهُ وَيُبَشِّرَ الْمُؤْمِنِيْنَ الَّذِيْنَ
يَعْمَلُوْنَ الصّٰلِحٰتِ اَنَّ لَهُمْ اَجْرًا حَسَنًا ۞ مَّاكِثِيْنَ فِيْهِ

<<All Praise is due to Allah, Who has revealed the Holy Book of the Qur'an to His Servant <Prophet Muhammad peace be upon him> **making this Holy Book perfect, without flaws, contradictions and crookedness** *[i.e., none of the verses contradict each other in any way]*

Allah Praised Himself for giving this Holy Book to His Prophet and made its contents and adherence to this Holy Book a cause for whoever follows it to be among the winners in the Hereafter. >> (18:1)

<< 'Qayyiman' means—This Perfect book is entirely accurate with verses that support and confirm each other in accuracy, to warn <the disbelievers> **of severe torture from Him.**

[God is not a body that lives in any place because God exists Eternally without a beginning, and He is Everlasting without death/destruction. The verse 'From Him' means, 'God will create for the disbelievers a severe torture as compensation for their blasphemy and lies.']

This blessed Holy Book is a source for some people to receive guidance to the truth. God revealed the good news to the Believers—those who do good deeds will have a tremendous

reward <, i.e., Paradise>. >> **(18:2)**

أبدا ۝ وينذر الذين قالوا اتخذ الله ولدا ۝ ما لهم به من
علم ولا لآبائهم كبرت كلمة تخرج من أفواههم إن
يقولون إلا كذبا ۝ فلعلك باخع نفسك على آثارهم إن لم
يؤمنوا بهذا الحديث أسفا ۝ إنا جعلنا ما على الأرض زينة
لها لنبلوهم أيهم أحسن عملا ۝ وإنا لجاعلون ما عليها
صعيدا جرزا ۝ أم حسبت أن أصحاب الكهف والرقيم
كانوا من آياتنا عجبا ۝ إذ أوى الفتية إلى الكهف فقالوا ربنا
آتنا من لدنك رحمة وهيئ لنا من أمرنا رشدا ۝ فضربنا
على آذانهم في الكهف سنين عددا ۝ ثم بعثناهم لنعلم أي

<<In which the believers will dwell in the reward that they earned>> (18:3) *Living in Paradise forever without termination.*

<<And Allah warns of severe torture to the blasphemers, especially these three groups, who claim, "Allah has an offspring.">> (18:4) *Those groups are—some Arab Pagans who said, 'Angels are the daughter of God,' the Jews who said, 'Ezra is the son of God,' and the Christians who said, 'Jesus is the son of God.'*

<<Those who attributed a child (i.e., son or daughter) **to God. They did not speak about such matters from prior knowledge but from their Excessive Ignorance,**

[It is mentally impossible for the Creator to have a child—Allah is not a child of parents (does not inherit), and He is not a father of children, nor is He inherited. It is extreme Atheism (Blasphemy) to believe God is the origin of the Universe, the Universe or part of the Universe, or God is the substance or matter of the Universe

or the essence of existence.] **Nor did their forefathers have the correct belief in God. They, too, were Excessively Ignorant. What an enormous blasphemous claim that comes out of their mouths!** *[Allah named them blasphemers for attributing to Allah what does not befit Allah, the Exalted]*

They attribute lies to Allah >> *[They fell into blasphemy because they did not use their sound mind; they used their excessive ignorance, but Allah did not excuse them for speaking nothing but blasphemy and lies.]* **(18:5)**

[When the Makkans rejected Prophet Muhammad's call to Islam—Allah revealed this Ayah to relieve his Prophet] <<**Now, you <O Prophet Muhammad> may grieve over their denial if they <continue to> disbelieve in this < Qur'an>.** >> **(18:6)**

<<God has indeed made available what is suitable on Earth from among its ornaments and its recommended usage, to 'Test them' [Allah's Knowledge encompasses everything—nothing can hide from God, so this test is not for God.]

This test will expose the people who among them will do good deeds>> *God will compensate the good doers with reward in the Afterlife and compensate the evildoers with torture in the Afterlife. *Everlasting torture is the only compensation to anyone who dies on blasphemy.* **(18:7)**

And God will certainly reduce what remains on it <the Earth closer to Judgment Day> **will turn to barren ground with no plants, trees, or vegetation.** >> *All the animals will die, and all the plants from trees and fruits will shrivel up and die.* **(18:8)**

<<Has your nation <O Muhammad> thought about the People of the Cave who slept a very long time and Ar-Raqeem, were they <the only> wonders of Our Signs? >>

This Ayah means O nation of Muhammad, the creation of the seven skies, Earth, and what is in them is more wondrous and impressive than the sign of the People of the Cave. 'Ar-Raqeem'—is a plaque at the cave entrance where the youths slept for 309 years. Some scholars said 'Ar-Raqeem' is the name of the mountain. Others said, 'It's the name of the valley where the cave is.' Some said, 'It's the name of the village of the People of the Cave,' and there are other sayings. **(18:9)**

<<Remember when those youths sought shelter in the cave? *They were Muslim Youths who were under supervision by their people. The Roman Emperor Dakianos ordered these youths to worship idols, which is blasphemy. So, these youths ran away to protect their Islamic Faith and hid in this cave. They spent their time supplicating to God through invocation, pleading, and prayer.*

They said, "Our Lord! Grant us Your Mercy and grant us protection, safety, and blessings against our enemies and create for us all that we need of guidance *[to escape the blasphemers and keep us steadfast on Islam]* **and facilitate for us ease to obey You and do the Good deeds that You will**

accept so we can achieve success and be on the right path. ">> (18:10)

<<**So, God cast** <created for these youths> **upon their ears a cover to sleep** <deeply> **in the cave for a specified many years** <309 years>. >> **(18:11)** *The Qur'an provides another astonishing example of science by mentioning hearing concerning sleep. Recent scientific discoveries state that hearing is the last sense to fall asleep and the first to awaken. All Praise is due to Allah!*

God revealed in the Holy Qur'an, Surat-ul-Anbiya' (The Prophets) Verse 1 means, <<**The time of the people's judgment has come so near, yet they heed not, and they turn away.** >>

Prophet Muhammad, peace be upon him, said,

"When you do At-Tashahhud in Salat Prayer, seek protection from your lord from 4 things: 'O Allah I seek refuge in you from the torture of Hellfire, and from the torture of the grave, and the seduction and temptation of life and death; and from the evil lure and temptation of Massih Ad-Dajjal (Antichrist).'"

[Allahumma inniy aʒoudhu bika min ʒadhabi Jahannam wa min ʒadhabil qabri wa min fitnat-il mahya wal mamati wa min sharri fitnat-il massih ad-Dajjal.]

CHAPTER 5

MAJOR SIGN NO. 2

Prophet Jesus Descends From the Second Sky

WHEN DAJJAL ARRIVES AND falsely claims Godhood, the number of people on this Earth who will worship him will be outrageous. Most people on Earth will fall into his evil lure and worship him invalidly. He is a disgraceful temptation, lure, and test to humanity and the most wicked human ever to exit. Tragically, most of humanity (billions) will fail this test.

The exact time of Prophet Jesus's descent is unknown. We know Jesus will descend at the Eastern side of Damascus at the white minaret. Two angels will escort him down to Earth with his hands resting on their wings.

Prophet Muhammad, peace be upon him, described this minaret before there was one in Eastern Damascus. This minaret exists today as defined by the Messenger of Allah; peace be upon him. The minaret is a light post for the new airport in Eastern Damascus.

Upon his descent, Prophet Jesus will travel to Jerusalem to the Aqsa Mosque. On arrival, he finds the Muslims gathered to pray the Dawn Prayer and a person makes Iqaamah for the Guided Ruler to lead the Dawn (Fajr) prayer.

Al-Mahdiyy, upon seeing Prophet Jesus entering the mosque, he will step back for Prophet Jesus to lead them all in the Salat Prayer. However, Prophet Jesus put his honorable hand on Mahdiyy's back, gently suggesting he step up and lead.

> Prophet Jesus will tell him, **"The Iqaama i.e.,** The Call for prayer indicting the prayer will begin immediately—**was made for you** (Al-Mahdiyy), **so you lead this Prayer."**

This occasion where a Prophet follows a Waliyy in prayer is the only time Prophet Jesus follows a Waliyy (Sufi) in Salat Prayer because prophets are much higher in rank than any Waliyy Sufi. Prophet Jesus, peace be upon him, followed the Mahdiyy during the dawn prayer to show he will rule by the Holy Qur'an and not the Holy Injeel. Although he received his divine laws over 2000 years ago, the revelation of the Holy Qur'an abrogated all previous Holy Books.

Prophet Jesus, upon his return, will follow, teach, and govern under the laws given to Prophet Muhammad, peace be upon them. Prophet Jesus will speak Arabic, although his original mother tongue is Syriac.

Since Prophets are the highest in the status of any Waliyy, Prophet Jesus will lead all the Salat prayers after that specific incident. After praying the Fajr (Dawn) prayer in congregation, Prophet Jesus will demand the door of the Aqsa Mosque to open. There, he will see Ad-Dajjal outside the door with

70,000 Jewish followers.

> Prophet Mu<u>h</u>ammad, peace be upon him, said, **"Upon seeing Prophet Jesus, Ad-Dajjal will dissolve like salt dissolves in water."**

Ad-Dajjal will attempt to escape. However, Prophet Jesus, peace be upon him, will tell Ad-Dajjal, **"I will have an opportunity to kill you, and I won't miss."** God will grant Prophet Jesus this opportunity at Baab Al-Ludd on the East side of Palestine. He will successfully kill Ad-Dajjal, ridding the world of his massive (fitnah) transgression and ending his blasphemy on Earth.

God will grant Prophet Jesus peace be upon him, a unique miracle, an ability to kill the non-believers from a distance—as far as he can see by exhaling (breathing out). He will kill the pig as it is an evil animal and very filthy najis meat, an enormous sin to consume. And Jesus will also demolish and break the cross because it symbolizes blasphemy, invalid worship, and lies against him and God.

Why will Prophet Jesus Returns to Earth?

Reason #1: All that comes from the Earth shall die and return to the Earth; Prophet Jesus is human, and although he has been living with Angels for the last 2000 years in the second sky, he must return to Earth to die and buried in the Earth at a prescribed time.

Reason #2: When Prophet Jesus first received revelation for being a Prophet and Messenger, God gave him a new Holy Book called—Al-Injeel and ordered him to teach Islam to his Israelites people—from the ancestors and children of Prophet Jacob, peace be upon him.

Prophet Jacob, also known as 'Isra'el,' was never Jewish or Zionist or had any blasphemous beliefs. Like all the Prophets before and after him, Prophet Jacob was always a Muslim who believed correctly in Allah. He taught the Israelites the same faith in God explicitly detailed in this book and in "Sacred Veil: Revealing Authentic Islam."

How Does Prophet Jesus believe in God? 13 Perfect Attributes:

1. ***God's Existence is Eternal*** *without being confined or limited to any place(s). God is not everywhere and is not in Heaven and not on the Grand Throne or above the Throne. God is not a body that Descends and Ascends during the night, as the fake Muslim Wahhabi hijackers have claimed.*

2. ***God is indivisible*** *without being attributed to any body—not a physical, tangible, or nontangible body. God is unimaginable—He does not have a body of any kind. He is not divisible and is not composed of the 3 in 1 false concept.*

3. ***God's Existence is Eternal without beginning.*** *God is dissimilar in every way from the entire universe that He created. God has never been in annihilation because He has always been existing. However, all creations were in complete annihilation and non-existence before God created them, proving no creation is worthy of Godhood.*

4. ***God's Existence is Everlasting without an end.*** *No one but God has an Everlasting Life that is uncreated. The limited lifespan of all humans, filled with weaknesses, makes them undeserving of Godhood. For he who is dead cannot create.*

5. ***God is dissimilar to anything on Earth and in this universe.*** *His Perfect Attributes are unlike any Humans, Jinns, Angels, or animals. God is uncreated and Exists without limits - without places, spaces, the six directions, or time. God is beyond human perception or imagination and is incomparable to humans. Hence, the concept that humans are created in God's image is entirely false and 100% blasphemy.*

6. ***God's Eternal Life is uncreated without spirit, offspring, partners, organs, limbs, or instruments.***

7. ***God's Eternal Hearing is uncreated*** *without limits or an ending. God hears all that is hearable simultaneously without organs, instruments, or sound waves.*

8. ***God's Eternal Sight is uncreated*** *without limits. God sees all that is seeable simultaneously without organs,*

instruments, or light.

9. ***God's Eternal Speech is uncreated and unlike any earthly speech*** *known to humanity. The speech of God is not languages, sounds, letters, words, or sentences.*

10. ***God's Eternal Knowledge is uncreated, all-encompassing, and never changes*** *– God's Knowledge does not increase or decrease. His Knowledge is Perfect.*

11. ***God is the only All-Powerful Creator who is uncreated.*** *Allah alone creates everything that comes into existence, whether good or evil - it all exists because God, the Creator, created it.*

12. ***God's Eternal Will is uncreated.*** *No creation can will something into existence that God has eternally willed its non-existence. No amount of praying or donating for the sake of God can change God's Eternal Will. What God has destined to be, it's impossible for any creation to stop or oppose His Eternal Will. If something exists, it is because God created it.*

13. ***God does not need anyone or anything*** *and does not require help or benefit from any creation. Believers do not benefit God, and disbelievers do not harm God.*

How was Prophet Jesus Risen?

Before the ascension of Prophet Jesus, peace be upon him,

to the second sky; he was on Earth for three years teaching Islam. During his life on Earth, there was no such person as a Christian who worshiped Jesus—present-day Christianity was non-existent in the life of Prophet Jesus on Earth.

During those three years—the Jews of that time saw his popularity and followers increasing, so they plotted to kill him like they killed criminals on a cross to maintain their power and stronghold on the people and the land. But Allah Eternally had a grander plan to Protect His Prophet and divert the harm away from him.

> Ibn Abi Hatim and An-Nasa'iyy related that Ibn ˆAbbas said, **'Jesus was with twelve of his companions in a house, and he said, "There are among you those who will commit heresy after believing. Who among you will choose to be made to look like me and killed in my place, then become my companion in Paradise?"**

The youngest among them stood up and said, **"It is I."** Jesus repeated his question.
The youngest again stood up and said, **"It is I,"** after Jesus repeated the question a third time, and the same young man said, 'Me,' Prophet Jesus, the son of Maryam, declared, **"You are the one."**

Before Jesus ascended to the second sky, God created the student of Prophet Jesus to have a likeness to Jesus.

Prophet Jesus physically ascended into the heavens from the last gathering through a rooftop window witnessed by his followers.

When the Jews arrived, they took the young man to kill and crucify, assuming he was Jesus. In the Qur'an, God exposed the doubt surrounding the authenticity of Jesus' death.

In another verse, God revealed in the Holy Qur'an that some Jews back then were boasting and making fun that they killed God's Prophet. So, the return of Jesus is God revealing the truth to the world—the Jews who bragged about killing Jesus did not kill him.

How will the Christians React?

When Prophet Jesus arrives in the coming years, many Christians will convert to Islam upon hearing Prophet Jesus's order not to worship him but to worship Allah alone without associating with God, partners, or a son.

> Prophet Jesus will order everyone to become Muslim because he is a Muslim and will tell the masses to say the Shahada—***The 2 Testifications of Faith—No one is God but Allah and Muhammad is the Messenger of Allah.***

Approximately 600 years before the birth of Prophet Muhammad, Prophet Jesus received the revelation of the

Holy Book called—Al-Injeel and conveyed its message to his people. However, upon his return, Prophet Jesus will govern the entire world by the Holy Qur'an because he is fully aware that the Holy Injeel and all other Holy Books became abrogated when the Qur'an was revealed.

Life After Ad-Dajjal's Death

Prophet Jesus kills the Imposter with his own hands. Afterward, life on Earth will be glorious for seven years, with everyone having strong faith, honesty, abundance, and prosperity. No person will have enmity against another.

God will bestow upon life great luxury, prosperity, blessings, safety, and pleasurable worship. In the era of Prophet Jesus, peace be upon him; life will be full of blessings and joy as everyone on Earth will be Muslim. The world will have no aggression, and even the wild animals will be peaceful. Safety will encompass the Earth because of the blessings of Prophet Jesus.

> Prophet Muhammad said, "<Safety will return to Earth> **so that the lions graze with the camels, the tigers graze with the cows, the fox grazes with the sheep, and the boys play with the snakes without harming them. Allah will remove the poisons from the snakes."**

In a Prophetic Hadith, peace be upon him, he said, **"Money would become plentiful to the extent no one will need it. Adding to their luxurious life, the joy and pleasure they encounter with every prostration they perform to Allah. Prosperity will engulf the land, and abundant wealth and fortune will be within reach for every Muslim. The Earth will release all its gold and treasures, making all the people living rich to the extent that there will be no one in need of charity."** Known as—Sadaqah—i.e., Money donated to the impoverished and needy.

> Prophet Muhammad, peace be upon him, in a Hadith classified as Sahih, in describing Prophet Jesus, said, **"He has an olive complexion, and of medium height and build, and has straight hair."**

Prophet Jesus, peace be upon him, will spend 40 years on Earth, and he will marry and have offspring. After his death, Muslims will perform the funeral prayer and bury him in the exact spot of his death next to the Chamber of Prophet Muhammad. As per the prophecy, peace be upon them all.

In Prophetic Hadith, peace be upon him, said, **"Wherever God wills for prophets to die, the Muslims bury them in the exact spot."** This location is currently vacant for Prophet Jesus; peace be upon him.

As for Prophet Jesus's descent to Earth, Al-Hakim related that the Messenger of Allah, peace be upon him, said, **"(Prophet) Jesus, the son of Mary will descend onto Earth as a ruler and a fair judge. He will perform Hajj or ʌUmrah and travel to visit my grave to salute me, and I will reply to his salutation."**

CHAPTER 6

MAJOR SIGN NO. 3

The Emergence of Gog and Magog

PROPHET JESUS WILL LIBERATE Muslims from Gog and Magog by traveling with the believers to Mount Tur in Egypt since the two nations are too many to kill. The believers will go to Egypt, where they will supplicate to God to relieve them of the barbaric disbelievers. The goal of Gog and Magog is to take over the Earth and kill its inhabitants. (Sounds familiar, does it not?)

Who Are the Nations of Gog & Magog?

The Prophet, peace be upon him, mentioned these barbarian nations live a long time. They die when they have witnessed 1000 or more of their offspring.

These two human tribes are descendants of Yafith, one of the three sons of Prophet Noah. They are all accountable blasphemers who are deathly evil.

When they eventually break through the iron partition, this overwhelming vast population will emerge, invading the inhabitants of this Earth with tremendous calamities. The nations of Gog and Magog have been alive, imprisoned, and isolated from other humans for thousands of years by God's Will in an unknown place on Earth.

Separating their overwhelmingly massive number from the rest of the Earth is a vast iron, copper, and lead wall that a very pious Muslim Sufi built named Dhul-Qarnayn.

Holy Qur'an mentions Dhul-Qarnayn and what he did to isolate these evil nations. The wall is solid and extensive, making it impossible for anyone living behind it to climb over it. However, it is believed that one day, they will be able to find a way to break through it and escape with the help of Allah's Will.

Who is Dhul-Qarnayn?

The following story comes from details found in verses in the Holy Qur'an. Dhul-Qarnayn, may Allah raise his rank, was a great Yemeni King and a pious man (Waliyy). Allah gave him many extraordinary matters called karamahs, and what he did with Gog and Magog is in the Holy Qur'an.

Some Scholars said his name was as-Saˆb, son of Al-Harith, and others said his name was as-Saˆb, son of Dhi Mara'ed. He was the most famous among the Yemeni Kings, the *Tababiˆah* of that era.

> One of his grandsons recited a poem about him saying: **My grandfather Dhul Qarnayn was**

> **an undefeated Muslim King. He traveled from east to west, acquiring reign over all the lands, as God granted to him, the Generous Lord.**

According to Muslim scholars, Prophet Al-Khadir led Dhul-Qarnayn's army as commander. Dhul-Qarnayn encountered Prophets Abraham and Isma^eel, peace be upon them, on his journey by foot from Yemen to Makkah for Hajj.

When Prophet Abraham, peace be upon him, learned of his arrival, he greeted him, made du^ah for him, and gave him general advice and guidance. Dhul-Qarnayn circumambulated the Ka^bah in Hijaz and sacrificed animals with Prophets Abraham and his son Isma^eel.

As a gesture of reverence, Dhul-Qarnayn declined the offer of a horse made by Prophet Abraham, stating, "I will not mount a horse in the land of Prophet Abraham." He was humble and did not want to appear superior, elevated in the land where Prophet Abraham lived, who was more honorable than him.

God revealed to Prophet Abraham to convey to Dhul-Qarnayn that Allah commanded the wind to take him wherever he wanted as a special blessing. A Karamah given to a Waliy (Sufi).

Allah Granted Dhul-Qarnayn Many Remarkable Matters:

- **A long life** and victory

- **Knowledge of different landmarks** and features of the Earth; as a result, he conquered numerous cities and ruled lands ranging from the East to the West.
- **Mastered different languages** and could communicate with the people he ruled in their native language. He was a compassionate king who ruled wisely. The inhabitants of the land he entered embraced Islam and were safe and prosperous, while those who refused were dishonored and shamed.
- **Illumination and darkness** were also under his command by the will of Allah. If he traveled at night, the path ahead would illuminate while the way behind him would remain dark. The darkness was a powerful weapon he used against his enemies. Darkness would engulf them on all sides, forcing them to retreat. On another occasion, he used the dark during his journey westward to the land of the setting sun.

Dhul-Qarnayn found a nation living there with murderers and unjust people spreading misguidance. He offered them extreme punishment in this world or reward in the Garden of Eden if they believed in God and performed good deeds. Dhul-Qarnayn stayed with them for a period, spreading guidance and goodness.

Dhul-Qarnayn desired to travel to uncharted lands nearer to where the sun rises after being near where the sun sets. Upon arriving, he found a vast, empty plain without construction, mountains, or trees. He found bizarre people who would escape the sun's intense heat at sunrise by hiding in dug-out burrows or diving underwater.

After the sunset, they would emerge again. Once, a group of soldiers arrived in this area and set up a camp close to these people. The residents advised the soldiers to avoid being on the land during sunrise to ensure their visitors' safety. Despite persuasion, the army insisted on staying until the sun rose.

When the army asked about the bones, the resident tribe told them, "These are the skeleton bones of another army who died when the sun rose over them some time ago." The army quickly fled upon hearing the news and seeing the evidence. Dhul Qarnayn observed the strange matter and, with Allah's aid, continued to conquer many lands.

He arrived in a valley between two mountains inhabited by two tribes. One spoke an incomprehensible, strange language. The neighboring tribes were evil and villainous nations called Gog and Magog.

Upon realizing Dhul Qarnayn was a mighty King, the tribe in the valley requested his help to build a separation barrier between them and the evil neighboring tribes. Dhul-Qarnayn agreed to help them.

Despite being offered payment for his service, Dhul-Qarnayn refused, stating, "What Allah has given me is worth more than what you offer. I only ask that you help me with the labor and machinery needed to build this partition."

They fulfilled his request by bringing him big iron slabs, each weighing a Qintar, which is about 110 lbs. He started at the bottom and reached the peak by placing iron blocks between the two mountains. He ignited the iron sheets with charcoal and wood, then told them to stoke the fire and blow on it to increase the heat. The fire melted the iron blocks. He poured liquid copper and lead onto the iron, which made a solid, smooth barrier that extended from the valley to the top of the mountains.

The iron barrier, similar to a mountain, was as high as 250 Dhiraˆ, equal to 125 meters. The surface was glass-smooth, making climbing impossible because there were no protrusions or holes. When Dhul-Qarnayn completed building the barrier, he said, "Allah facilitated this for us by His mercy. God will destroy this wall when the Day of Judgment is near."

Imprisoning Gog and Magog behind this iron mountain barrier:

Every day since its erection, the nations of Gog and Magog attempt to break through the barrier but fail. Every day, they tirelessly work a long, strenuous day trying to break through. They say, "Tomorrow, we will continue." However, to their dismay, they come back the next day only to find the small hole that they had made resealed.

They continue attempting to dig their way out of the barrier daily. However, one day, closer to Judgment Day, when Prophet Jesus, peace be upon him, has returned to Earth for his second coming. God will inspire one of them to say, "Tomorrow, God-willing, we will continue"– i.e., this person is seeking God's support, although he is a blasphemer.

The following day, they will find the hole they dug has remained intact, unlike other days and years before. This day marks when this expansive nation will resume digging through the tunnel from where they stopped and finally emerge through the broken barrier to disperse across the planet.

Their emergence will be the third major sign indicating Judgment Day is nearing. May Allah protect us from their terrors and awes.

Dhul-Qarnayn, a rare, just king, lived for two thousand years, ruling and teaching fairness in alignment with Islamic law. He died armed with many good deeds and righteousness prepared for the Hereafter.

Most Earthly Kings perish as unjust rulers, utterly bankrupt of any good deeds on Judgment Day.

Gog & Magog Invade the Earth...

There are false stories claiming these nations are midgets with huge ears. They use one ear as a pillow and the other as a blanket. Those claims are untrue.

Their release will devastate the rest of Earth as a famine on Earth will occur. As they come down from elevated mountain tops, they will be like swarms towards the people and land–eating and destroying everything in their path.

The Messenger of Allah, peace be upon him, described two nations of God and Magog as having **'Small eyes, wide faces with more white head-hair than black. They are brutal warriors who live a long time, long enough to see one thousand or more offspring.'**

> The Prophet, peace be upon him, said, **"The population of Gog and Magog, since their isolation, have been dramatically increasing in number from thousands of years ago. They are such a massive population that on Judgment Day, the ratio of Gog and Magog compared with the regular humans will be a hundred to one. (100:1)"**
>
> And in another narration, **"One thousand of them to one of us. (1000:1)"**

They will approach a deep lake called **'Tabarayya'** in Palestine, which is so deep it is called 'bottomless.' When the last person from Gog and Magog reaches the water bank to drink, he will say, **"There once was water here."** They drink it all, leaving nothing.

Since they cannot kill the overwhelming number of Gog and Magog and free the lands, Prophet Jesus, peace be upon him, and Allah will command the Muslims to journey to the blessed Mount of at-Tur in Egypt. This is the same holy mountain where Prophet Moses received his Prophetic Revelation.

The Muslims will be stuck on the mountaintop when they reach the summit, unable to go down because of Gog and Magog swarming the mountain's base.

The summit will leave Muslims without food and water, causing them to seek relief from God and pray for victory over the savage nations as promised. They pray to Allah for relief and triumph from the calamity of Gog and Magog, and God answers their prayers.

Allah will make worms descend onto the necks of all the people of Gog and Magog, entering their necks. They will all fall and die instantaneously as if one person died. Imagine if they are 700 billion people all dead.

The foul odor from their dead bodies will consume the Earth—God spares no place on Earth, not even six inches from their vile smell. The Muslims will plead in prayer to Allah to relieve them from their foul odor.

God sends unique birds to transport all the dead bodies to seas and oceans. Afterward, heavy rain will wash away the traces of the Nations of Gog and Magog into the sea, ridding the Earth of all nonbelievers.

These evil and devastating nations will appear after Prophet Jesus returns to Earth.

Are there unknown Nations on Earth after Gog and Magog?

On the Day of Judgment, God will remove the symbolic barrier from our hearing so that all the people will hear the Eternal Speech of God that is not a sound, letter, or any language metaphorically because there is no physical barrier to our ears.

If the Speech of God was letters, words, or sounds, how long would it have taken for the nations of Gog and Magog to be questioned? It would have taken thousands of years and an extended period. God created Satan before Prophet Adam, and he will not die until the Angel blows the horn before Judgment Day begins. If God's Speech were words, letters, and sound, Questioning Satan alone would have taken more than 50,000 years.

Will there be other nations?

Yes. Three nations will appear after Gog and Magog. Only God knows the whereabouts and number of these nations, Mansaku, Eyaweel, and Eyarees, on this Earth. The inhabitants of Earth will witness these blasphemer nations following the death of the Nations of Gog and Magog.

We all know that the Nations of Gog and Magog are

substantial—100 or 1000 of them to one of us. One of the 50 stages on the Day of Judgment is the stage of Hisaab, i.e., the Questioning of the Slaves. God will Question all humans and jinn briefly because God's Speech (Kalaam) does not resemble the Speech of Humans.

Humans have a beginning, so all their attributes and traits are created creations with a beginning, too. Human Speech is a creation that comprises letters, sounds, and languages.

> Imam Abu Hanifa said, **"Allah's Speech is not like our speech. We speak with organs and letters. Allah's Speech is unimaginable – without organs, instruments, letters, sounds or any language."**

Allah's Self differs from any created being. The Creator's Eternal Attributes are not like those of any creation, and God does not resemble any of His creations. Creation is a thing that possesses created qualities. The Creator is not a creation and does not have created attributes. God questions all of creation in a short amount of time.

On Judgment Day, all the Believers and nonbelievers will hear the Eternal Speech of Allah. The pious Muslims will be delighted to hear the Speech of God, while the blasphemer will feel anguish and annoyance. Aware of their suffering, everlasting misery, and torture, the Blasphemers will have no solace in death.

This Ayah is among the strongest proofs that the Eternal Speech of God is not letters, sounds, or any language – not Arabic, Hebrew, or Syriac.

Allah revealed about Himself in the Holy Qur'an, which means, <<**And He <God> is the fastest Reckoner (Questioner)**>> [Wahuwa asraˆoul Haasibeen]

Chapter 7

The Longest Living Human

Who is Al-Khadir?

AL-KHADIR IS THE LONGEST-LIVING human being alive today because of what he did thousands of years ago.

God granted Al-Khadir the most extended human life, and he continues to live today on Earth for as long as Allah wills for him.

> According to one narration, Al-Khadir is a direct offspring of Adam, peace be upon him. Other scholars have mentioned that he is Balya' bin Malkan, whose lineage goes back to Sam, son of Noah, peace be upon him.

According to both narrations, Al-Khadir was born before Prophet Abraham, peace be upon him. He was first cousins with Abraham's grandfather.

He was called *'Al-Khadir,'* derived from the Arabic word for green, as he once sat on a barren land that became lush with vegetation. Also known as Abul ^Abbas, wherever he prayed, the surrounding Earth would turn green by the Will of Allah, as an endowment from God showing his high rank in piety.

Prophet Muhammad, peace be upon him, conveyed that when Prophet Adam, peace be upon him, was on his deathbed, he warned his offspring of severe torture to come.

Prophet Adam summoned his children and said, **'O sons, Allah is going to inflict severe torture upon the people with a devastating flood.'** He conveyed his Will to carry his body with them on the Ark and then bury him in a specific cave near the area of ash-Sham.

Prophet Adam's last Will was transmitted from generation to generation until it reached Noah, who became a prophet. In a divine revelation to Prophet Noah, God revealed that water would trickle out of Eve's oven when the flood was coming soon.

Yes, this is the same Lady Eve and Prophet Adam who used to live and cook there prior. When Prophet Noah saw the sign that the flood would come, he loaded the Ark with two pairs of each animal.

Noah's Ark had three levels:

1. On the bottom were all the wild animals.
2. On the top level were all the birds.
3. On the middle level – The Ark carried only eighty individuals, including Prophet Noah and his three sons. Only these 80 people believed in God and

> survived the historical flood. They comprised 77 males and only three females who were the wives of Noah's three sons.

From the offsprings of these three women, all races on Earth populated again. Therefore, Muslim scholars say, 'Prophet Noah is your father after your father (Adam).'

Prophet Noah took Prophet Adam's body and carried it onboard the Ark with the people. Before the unusual rainfall descended, God ordered the Earth to expel its water and overflow until it submerged even the highest of mountains to protect them.

Afterward, for 40 days and nights, God created unusual rainfall the size of boulders that came down. If the mountains were not submerged, the distinctive rain would have obliterated them on impact.

Noah's Ark landed on Mt. Judiyy in Babylon (Iraq) six months after the floodwaters receded into the Earth. Prophet Noah requested his three sons, Sam, Ham, and Yafith, to transport Prophet Adam's body to the cave he had chosen as his burial place.

"The land is deserted and difficult to maneuver. We will lose our way and won't find it. Let us wait until there is a considerable population," his sons replied

Noah replied to encourage them, **"Adam supplicated that the person who buries him will live a very long life, close to**

Judgment Day."

The body of Prophet Adam, peace be upon him, was passed down by generations until Prophet Al-Khadir fulfilled Adam's request to move him into the final resting place in a cave.

As a result, Allah granted Al-Khadir a very long life, so he continues to live for as long as God willed.

Another Reason

Another reason for Al-Khadir's very long earthly life involves Dhul-Qarnayn, the Great! This story explains how Prophet Adam's supplication for a long life was granted to Al-Khadir.

Dhul-Qarnayn is not Alexander the Great, as some people suggest. Dhul-Qarnayn was a pious, righteous, God-fearing Muslim Waliy (Sufi) who owned vast lands stretching East to West.

An honored angel and righteous friend of Dhul-Qarnayn, Angel Rafaˆil, visited him occasionally.

Learning About 'The Fountain of Youth'...

While visiting with the honorable Angel Rafaˆil, Dhul-Qarnayn expressed his wish for a long life.

He said, **"O Rafaˆil, I hope Allah will extend my life so that I can excel in obeying and worshipping Him truly as He deserves."**

Rafaˆil inquired, **"Is this really what you would like?"**

Dhul-Qarnayn replied, **'Yes.'**

Rafaˆil said, **"There is a spring called the Spring of Life. God will grant the one who drinks from this spring longevity and a very long life only known to God."**

Dhul-Qarnayn eagerly asked, **"Do you know where this spring is?"**

"No, we angels talk about a dark place on Earth. None of us, or humans and jinns, have reached it. We think the Spring is there," Rafaˆil said. The angels discuss a dark place Allah created on Earth, speculating the Spring is there.

Dhul-Qarnayn consulted the Muslim Scholars regarding the *'Spring of life,' i.e., 'The Fountain of Youth,'* and they said they had never heard of it.

He asked, **"During your studies, were any of you taught Allah created a dark place?"**

"Why do you ask?" responded the scholar.

Dhul-Qarnayn disclosed Angel Rafaˆil's message.

The scholar responded he read about this ominous place in Adam's Will, and it is in the East where the sun rises.

Dhul-Qarnayn chose 2000 horsemen for his army to search for the *Water of Life* and appointed Al-Khadir, peace be upon him, as their commander.

They traveled for 12 years until they reached a valley at the edge of darkness, only to find that it was not darkness caused by night but by heavy fog.

Needing to make Wudu' for prayer, Al-Khadir halted the army briefly to descend on his own towards the valley.

There, he found himself at the edge of a spring, so he took off his clothes only to find that the water was whiter than milk and sweeter than honey. He drank from it, made Wudu', and bathed. He then put his clothes back on and returned.

The army, led by Dhul-Qarnayn, attempted to find the valley where Al-Khadir descended, but it was not God's Will for them to discover it. God endowed Dhul-Qarnayn to live a pious life on Earth, earning him many rewards for the afterlife.

To his great disappointment, Dhul-Qarnayn lost his way in the darkness and never found *the Spring of Life—The Fountain of Youth.*

Al-Khadir, peace be upon him, is an honorable Prophet whom God granted the longest life on Earth from all human beings.

He used to live amongst the people like the rest of the Prophets. But then, Allah made the water's surface like a walking ground for him—so he walks and lives on the water.

Al-Khadir lives alone on the sea's surface, hidden from the rest of humanity. Allah has made it so that only a select blessed few individuals can see him, while most people will never see him.

This Honorable Prophet might arrive at a location without knowing he ever came. God also endowed Prophet Moses to meet and see Al-Khadir and some great Waliys (Sufis).

Al-Khadir has been following God's orders and performing acts of obedience on Earth for thousands of years. Prophet Al-Khadir works unseen, helping and protecting Muslims worldwide, as God commands.

Chapter 8

Major Sign No. 4

Sun Rises from the West

The Final Hour is, without a doubt, a lot closer. Unlike all previous signs, A sign will occur after the Emergence of Dajjal, the Descend of Prophet Jesus back to Earth, and after Gog and Magog. This Sign will entirely change the situation of life on Earth. The signs before this Sign are not the same as the signs after this Sign.

> God made repentance from all sins, large and small, an obligation and the Qur'an orders it, **<< (God is ordering) Repent from all your sins O Believers>>** <wa tubu illallaahi jamiʌan Ay-yuhal Mu'minun>

The Prophet, peace be upon him, said, **"The (Muslim) person who says in the day, *'Subhan-Allahi wa bi hamdihi subhan-Allahil-Al-ˆAdheem'* their sins** (those sins that are less than blasphemy) **will erase even if the sins were as numerous as seafoam—i.e., billions of small sins".**

These are not sins of blasphemy because only the

Testifications of Faith will return such a person to Islam after committing blasphemy.

What is this Sign?

The Sun rises from its setting place.

The Sun rises from the east and sets in the West in a set system—this is how we are all accustomed to seeing the Sun. What about a day when all this changes? Yes, the Sun will rise from the western horizon.

The beloved of Allah, Prophet Muhammad, peace be upon him, said to one of his companions at sunset, **"Do you know where the sun goes when it reaches the extent of the West?"**

They said, "Allah and his messenger know best."

The Prophet, peace be upon him answered,

"The Sun goes until it reaches its setting place *(Mustaqar)*, **prostrates under the ˆArsh, and waits for permission to return. Then it gets permission to return to where it came from before."**

And the Sun rises on time every day. As you know, the Sun rises and sets daily for centuries and millennia—on time like clockwork.

Where is the Sun's Settlement place [Mustaqar]?

The Prophet, peace be upon him, said, **"Under the Grand Throne."** *[Taht-Al-ˆArsh]*

Where is the Grand Throne?

The Grand Throne is the ceiling of Paradise and is the vastest of all the creations that God created, and God did not create this Throne to sit on—no Muslim on the face of the Earth who believes that God is sitting on the Throne.

The people who believe God is sitting anywhere are not Muslims, even if they insist they are.

The Prince of the Believers, Imam and Master ˆAliy son of Abi Talib, may Allah reward him, the cousin and son-in-law of Prophet Muhammad said,

"Allah created the Grand Throne as a sign of His Power and did not create it as a place for Him to take <to sit on>."

What does this verse in Surat Taha mean? <<Ar-Rahmaan ˆalal-ˆArshi-stawaa>>

The true meaning of this verse is: <<**Allah controls the Throne**>> This verse does **not** mean Allah sits on the Throne, as so many false mistranslations blasphemously assert.

> **Al-Qahhaar** is among the 99 names of Allah, which means **"The One who has control over all his creations."** Allah controls and protects the Grand Throne from falling from its elevated place in the universe.

The word **'Al-Jaliss'**, which means, **'The one who sits.,'** is definitely **NOT** among the 99 names of Allah.

The Sun will Rise from the West.

The Sun travels its route and finishes by retiring at its settlement place under the Throne.

It stays in the prostration position until God orders it to rise from the eastern horizon daily. And the people will be surprised to see the Sunrise from the West.

The Prophet, peace be upon him, said,
"Every day, the Sun will rise and set on time as usual, and the people have no objection.

Then, one day, it will go to its place of setting and prostrate beneath the ˆArsh, which is the ceiling of Paradise. Then Allah will detain and keep it at that location until it is tardy.

The Sun will say, "O my Lord, I have delayed the people who wait for the Sun to rise."

On that day, God will give the sun permission to rise, but it will be said, "Rise, begin the dawn rising from where you came—the Western Horizon."

And the people will be surprised to see the sun rose from the west.

What does this Sign mean?

The Door of Repentance, open for thousands of years, has now closed.

Tirmidhiyy narrated that Prophet Muhammad peace be upon him said, **"In the western horizon, there is a door that God created for repentance. Its width is 70 years wide. It will only close once the Sun rises from it."**

> Allah revealed in Surat Al-An^am, verse 158 in the Holy Qur'an means,
> **"On the Day your Lord's signs arrive, belief will not benefit those who did not believe earlier (before this day) or those who did no good deeds through their faith (before that day)"**
> *[<Yawma ya'tiy ba^Du ayaati rabbik laa yanfa^ou nafsan emanuha lam takun amanat min qablu aw kasabat fi imanuha khayra>]*

The Prophet, peace be upon him, said about this verse, **"This is when the sun rises from the West."**

[dhalika hina tatlu^ ash-shamsu min maghribihaa]

What does this Ayah (Verse) mean?

Any blasphemer will not benefit from believing and wanting

to have faith after the Sun rises from the Western horizon. Any sinner Muslim believer would not benefit from doing good deeds if they did not do any good deeds before the Sun rose on the Western horizon.

> **Why?** *God has rules for accepting faith and doing good deeds; when the Sunrises from the West, the disbelievers will be similar to seeing the angel of death when it is too late for belief to be accepted.*

Allah said in the Qur'an in Surat An-Nisaa verse 18, what means, <<**However, Repentance will not be accepted from those who <knowingly> persist on sinning until they see the Angel of Death and then cry, 'I repent now.' And for those who die as blasphemers, We (God) have prepared a painful punishment.>>**

[Wa layssat attawbatu lilladhina yaʌmalouna sayyi'aat hattaa idha 7adara ahadahumul mawt qaala inni tubtul aan...walal ladhina yamoutoon wa hum kuffar dhalika laa yufido shay'aa...]

As God revealed in the Qur'an in Surat Ghafir, verse 85 that means, <<**But their faith was no benefit to them when they saw the Angel of Death. The disbelievers were at a 'Total' loss.>>**

[Fa lam yaku yanfaˆuhum Emanuhum lamma ra'ou ba'sanaa]

The chance to repent is open for you and everyone on Earth until the Sun rises from the West. The status of everyone's achievements before Sunrise on that day will separate the believers from the blasphemers.

Did the Muslims gain good deeds before that day?

Did the Muslims repent from their enormous sins before that day?

Did the nonbelievers embrace Islam and believe in God correctly before this day?

On that day, God will accept no one's repentance - not the sinner Muslims or the blasphemers. *[wa kufiyal ˆamal].*

To all of you who are drowning in sin,

To all of you who are hopeful of this perishing world,

To all of you who thoroughly forget about death,

To all of you who sin and indulge yourself in the pleasure of this world,

Remember: "The person who disobeys Allah while laughing, God enters them into Hellfire on Judgment Day while they cry. The person who obeyed Allah while crying, God enters them into Paradise on Judgment Day while they are laughing."

Life on Earth is not a permanent residence, but God made this earthly life a temporary passageway and not a permanent home.

The Prophet urged us to use this life to gain reward for the afterlife.

Remember, you can run away from your mother and father, your sister and brother, an unjust ruler trying to harm you or run away from your wife to whom you shelter, and she shelters you.

But where is the escape from death?

Death that most people seek to avoid will reach you one day.

Take heed of your ignorance and your evil actions.

The Sun will rise from the Western Horizon, and the Door of Repentance will close shut.

There is no way to repent after this Major Sign.

The enormous sinners cannot repent from their enormous sins, and the blasphemers cannot embrace Islam.

What comes after today will be different from what came before today. An incredibly frightening sign this will be! What a significant marker this day will be. May Allah bless us with repentance and the strength never to repeat our sins.

We ask Allah to erase all of our sins, O Lord. You are All-Powerful, and we (creations) are all weak. Have mercy upon us and forgive us and our weaknesses, O Allah.

O Allah. Your forgiveness is greater than our sins. I am more hopeful of Your Mercy than my deeds.

Forgive me, O Allah.

By Allah, Judgment Day is near

Are you prepared?

Chapter 9

Major Sign No. 5

The Earth Beast

THE CLEAR AND POWERFUL sign witnessed on this day will make every person believe in the truth, in Islam, and in Allah. Belief in Allah only on the day of the Major Sign, without belief the day before, will not be accepted by God. Once the Door of Repentance is closed, God will not accept the repentance from anyone.

> God revealed in the Qur'an what means, **<<The day when there shall come some of the signs of your Lord, O Muhammad. No soul shall benefit from its faith on that day.>>** If that soul had not previously believed.

When the sun has risen the length of a spear, approximately 20 minutes after it rises from the Western Horizon, **'Duha'** begins. A beast will speak with the people, and no one can prevent what God orders it to do. God is powerful over all things.

Allah revealed it in the Qur'an in verse 82 of Surat an-Naml (Ants) means, <<**When the Hour's decree befalls them, an Earth beast will come to them saying that people had no faith in Our <Holy> Verses.**>>

God punishes the world for its widespread sins and offers relief through repentance.

Globally, most people will severely disobey God and not believe in Islam. Most people will not adhere to the Islamic laws, the verses of the Qur'an, or the religious rules. At that time, God will send the people on Earth an animal called **Dabbatul Ard—' The Earth Beast.'**

What does the phrase mean in the Holy Verse <<**Waqa^al Qawlu ^aleyhim**>>?

This Ayah means <<**The Decree that God has promised becomes necessary to fall upon those who transgressed in their tyranny and sinning**>>.

What is the Earth Beast?

The Muslim scholars do not have a consensus on who this Earth Animal will be. Some Scholars said, **'It is the Baby Camel that returned inside the Boulder'** after the misguided people from the Nation of Prophet Salih killed the mother camel.

One of the miracles that God gave Prophet Salih was two live camels—a mother and a baby came out of a massive boulder after his people requested this exact miracle. However, only some of his people believed in God and his Prophethood afterward, but most did not.

When the non-believers conspired and savagely killed the mother camel, the baby camel ran back inside the same boulder. *(Detailed story inside the New Release coming January 2024: "SACRED PROPHETS: Chronicles of Divine Revelation")*

Some Scholars said, **'It is the Jassassa animal that was on the island with Ad-Dajjal.'** *Other scholars said other than that.*

From Where will this Beast Come?

> God revealed what means, <<**When the time comes, Allah shall bring forth to them a beast from the Earth that shall speak to them that the people were not certain about the signs of Allah.**>>

The Prophet said, **"After the Earth Beast comes out, it will shake the dirt off its head."**

There is no consensus from Muslim Scholars as to which location the Earth Beast will come from however, they said about this large animal:

- It will exit from **Mount As-Safa in Makkah** causing the mountain to crumble for this beast to exit.
- It will exit from the **Koufah Mosque**, where the water trickled from Eve's oven during the time of Prophet Noah, peace be upon him.
- It will exit from the **Land of Ta'if.**
- It will exit from a **boulder in Aj-yaad, in Makkah.**

And other sayings...

The Ring of Prophet Solomon & the Staff of Moses

When it arrives, the Earth Beast will have in its possession—the ring of Prophet Solomon and the Staff of Prophet Moses; peace be upon them.

No one can escape this creature; it will catch every person. Its pursuit is so relentless no one can escape from it, and nobody can catch it if it runs. This creature will mark the face of every person it catches. If that person was, in fact, a disbeliever, the

Earth beast would mark his face, showing he is a disbeliever.

If the Earth Beast catches a genuine believer, it will cleanse (Tajlu) the faces of all the believing people, making their faces shine brighter. It will mark all the blasphemers' noses using Prophet Sulayman's ring. God knows the religious status of the people during that time and gives the Earth Beast the wisdom to know who is a believer and who is not. The Beast will move from place to place, performing its duties before departing.

Prophet Muhammad, peace be upon him, spoke of a man who would claim to be a Muslim and stand to perform the Salat prayer quickly when he saw the Earth Beast.

> The Earth Beast will confront and encircle him, saying, **"Now you are praying?"**

When he turns around upon hearing the question, the Earth Beast, before departing, will mark the man's face, showing he is, in fact, a blasphemer and not a Muslim.

People would address each other based on the signs on their faces. The believers and blasphemers will use the titles' Believer' and 'Disbeliever' to address each other.

> The Blasphemer will say, **'O Believer, give me my right'** [Iqdini Haqqi] and the Believer will

say, **"O Blasphemer, give me my right.'** [Iqdini Haqqi]

The Huge Door of Repentance will close that day, and a physical mark will distinguish the Believers from the Disbelievers. On that day, repentance will not be possible for anyone who was a disbeliever. Even the Muslim sinner cannot repent for his sins.

If any blasphemer wishes to become Muslim and says the Testifications of Faith, God will not accept him, so he cannot become Muslim. Once the door of repentance closes, repentance is no longer an option for a disbeliever or an enormous Muslim sinner.

The Door of Repentance is Wide Open

The *Door of Repentance* is wide open in the Western Horizon. It remains open until the day the sun rises from it in the West. The Earth Beast will emerge approximately 20 minutes after sunrise.

Judgment Day is closer and closer.

What if you are alive when the Earth Beast exits to place its mark on the people? Will your heart be able to handle it?

What will you do if you are alive when the sun rises in the West, and the Earth Beast marks your nose?

What if you knew you would surely die a blasphemer, and

there is no hope for you to repent after that?

This would mean you will die a disbeliever and be among the Dwellers of Hellfire on Judgment Day forever and ever.

Do you love to do good, and will God accept you?

Then, learn and become a real Muslim if you are not already before it is too late.

- Upon the masses becoming very ignorant of Islam, **corruption will spread on land and at sea.**
- When few people on Earth possess Islamic Knowledge, **God creates widespread calamities.**
- If Muslims do not order lawful deeds and forbid others from unlawful and sinful acts, **God afflicts the masses with calamities.**

Doesn't that sound like our world today?

These two Major signs occur very close together, in one day between Dawn and Duha (approximately 20 minutes after sunrise)—this one day will change life on Earth as we know it. From that day forward, God will not accept repentance from anyone.

Judgment Day is so much closer

> The Prophet, peace be upon him, in his lifetime said, **"Judgment Day and I were sent like this"** [Bu^ithtu ana was-saa^ah ka hatayn] **and the Prophet showed his index and middle finger parallel and touching one another.**

Judgment Day today is much closer than when the Prophet, peace be upon him, was alive on Earth almost 1,500 years ago. Will you consider its significance? Are you prepared? I recommend you get ready.

Chapter 10

Major Signs No. 6 - 9

Dense Smoke & Earthquakes

No.6. Dense Smoke

One of the major signs that Judgment Day is near will be smoke that will come down from the Sky and fill the entire Earth. God only knows what the source of this massive smoke will be.

It may not be artificial environmental pollution or an atomic explosion. Dense smoke will spread and travel, covering the entire Earth.

Some people will suffer the effect of suffocation to near death. In comparison, other people will only be mildly affected.

> God revealed in the Holy Qur'an what means, **<<Wait for the day when the Sky shall come with smoke, clear evident smoke that covers the people. They shall say, 'This is a painful torture.'>>**

The Prophet peace be upon him said, **"The smoke will come from the sky, blanketing the entire Earth for 40 days and nights."** And, he said, **"The smoke will affect the believers as though they have the symptoms of the common cold. However, the smoke will severely affect those who are not Muslim and feel like they're dying from suffocation. The smoke will enter their bodies and exit through all their orifices: mouth, nose, ears, and anus.**

This will be one of the Major Signs that
Judgment Day is drawing Near.
Are you getting ready?

After Allah destroys the entire nations of Gog and Magog, will more Major signs appear?

Yes. The *Kusoof.*

Not one, but three fissure earthquakes of colossal magnitude must come to pass.

7: A severe magnitude fissure earthquake within the Eastern Hemisphere of the Earth

8: The Earth's Western Hemisphere will have a massive fissure earthquake.

9: An enormous fissure earthquake in the Middle East.

In one year, three colossal landslides caused by massive earthquakes will occur - one in the East, one in the West, and one in the Arabian Peninsula.

What is a Fissure Earthquake?

> God revealed in the Qur'an what means,
> **<<They shall say, 'This is a painful torture.' Among them is the earth shall be cleft asunder in three different locations.>>**

This cleave means the Earth will split deeply, breaking open, separating and splitting the ground of the Earth, and swallowing all that is on its surface on a significant scale.

Although colossal earthquakes have occurred historically, these three earthquakes are prophecies.

God revealed these three signs as large signs to warn humanity that Judgment Day is near.

Therefore, these signs will cause tremendous catastrophic destruction, as each one will be its Major sign, so their magnitude will be destruction we have not witnessed before.

Allahu Akbar! God is Great!

The Prophet peace be upon him said,
"These indications will appear only when these areas reach their highest levels of immorality and wicked behavior (from its people)."

Umm Salama, the mother of the Believers, heard the Prophet, peace be upon him speaking about the *Kusoof* and asked, **"O Messenger of Allah, will this fissure quake occur in a place with righteous Muslims?"**

The Prophet, peace be upon him, answered,
"Yes, if most of its dwellers were malicious blasphemers."
[Idhaa aktharu ahluh-al-Khabath]

The Prophet, peace be upon him, said,
"Judgment Day will not come until a fissure quake (Kusoof) occurs to the Arab tribes (i.e., in the Middle East)."
[laa taqumus-saa^ah hatta yukhsaf bi qabaa'ila minal ^Arab]

Prophecy has predicted that three colossal earthquakes will occur in the same year. These quakes will cause large-scale death in three major areas on Earth, where disobedience, wickedness, and evil have reached a colossal peak.

Allahu Akbar! How devastating will these signs be? How many arrogant people will be swallowed alive? Judgment Day is very near. Are you prepared?

What Happens to the Muslims?

Allah will create a cold wind from the Levant countries known in the past as one country called '*Ash-Sham*' comprising *Lebanon, Syria, Palestine, and Jordan.*

A gentle and cold breeze will enter under the arms of every believer, causing all the believers on Earth to die. Death from this breeze is inevitable for anyone with the tiniest atom of faith. Per God's decree, no believer in God will live beyond this point. This breeze will enter and find the believer even within the confines of a small hidden cave in a faraway mountain. On that day, all Muslims will die from this breeze.

During one night, God will raise the Holy Qur'an so that no single letter or verse remains on Earth. The longest-living human, Prophet Al-Khadir, peace be upon him, is detailed in Chapter 7, will die on that night.

His age is well over seven thousand years old, and he will continue living until the last group of Muslims die on Earth, 100 years before the Earth's destruction.

The worst of the wicked disbelievers will only inhabit the

Earth in the last one hundred years. Blasphemers will spread evil, enmity, deceit, fear, and idol worship on this Earth. The blasphemers will witness the Earth's destruction before their inevitable demise.

In the last era on Earth, Prophet Muhammad, peace be upon him, prophesied that the least wicked blasphemers would commit adultery in the streets. In the last 100 years, no one will remember their Creator. Satan will order idol worship, and all remaining humans will be idol worshipers on Earth.

What Happens to the Holy Qur'an?

Peace be upon Prophet Moses who lived in the era of widespread sorcery and magic. When God ordered Prophet Moses to go to Pharaoh and order him to embrace Islam, Pharaoh called upon 1000 of his magicians to disprove Prophet Moses. The magicians deceived the on-lookers with false illusions, except the prophets. No magic can affect the eyes of any Prophet.

The magicians cast down their ropes and, by magic, caused the people to think they were seeing snakes. However, Prophet Moses cast down the staff God gave him, and it turned into a gigantic serpent, devouring a thousand ropes that had tricked the people.

Pharoah's Magicians immediately prostrated to God in Glorification and declared their belief in Prophet Moses, peace be upon him. The magicians embraced Islam because they were sure what they had witnessed was a miracle from God, not magic.

In the Qur'an, Allah swore by the Dawn (aD-Duha) in commemorating the blessed hour when Pharoah's Magicians embraced Islam. **All 1000 of his Magicians simultaneously believed in God and Prophet Moses; peace be upon him.**

Allah sent Prophet Jesus to his people—the Israelites—at a time in history when medicine was prevalent, so God gave Prophet Jesus numerous miracles that reflected his era. Some of Prophet Jesus's miracles are healing the blind and leper by the Will of God.

He used to wipe on the eyes of a person born blind, curing him. This illness is called *'Akmah'* in Arabic, and until today, medicine does not have a cure for this illness. But by the blessings and honor of Prophet Jesus, peace be upon him; God created the cure to sight by the hand of His honorable Prophet's wiping.

Allah sent His best and illiterate Prophet during an era of proficient Arabic linguists. Prophet Muhammad, peace be upon him, is God's best Prophet, and God honored him by making him illiterate. Prophet Muhammad's miracles reflected the era he lived in, which had many experts with exceptional skills in the Arabic language. The Prophet's inability to read and write was a divine honor, leading to the greatest miracle - the Holy Quran.

God gave revelation to his best and unlettered Prophet,

who surprised and defeated eloquent disbelievers. Prophet Muhammad, peace be upon him, could not have gained prophetic knowledge from reading books because he was illiterate.

How is it removed?

However, one day, God will remove this incredible miracle with all its blessed letters and words from all the hearts of people and all the pages of The Qur'an and raise it to the skies. Not a single verse from the Qur'an will remain anywhere on Earth, and that is when God will make Prophet Al-Khadir die, peace be upon him.

> Prophet Muhammad, peace be upon him said, **"The Holy Verses in the Qur'an in one night will be removed from the entire Earth—not one verse <ayah> will remain. And there will be a group of people, the old and elderly, who will say—we remember hearing our fathers saying this statement—No one is God but Allah."** These people will say this after the death of all the Muslim believers.

[Yusra ˆala kitabillahi fi laylatin fa laa yabqa fil-ardi minhu ayah wa tabqa tawa'ifu minnas—Ash-shaykhul kabiru wal ˆajuzu yaquluna 'adrakna aba'ana ˆala hadhihil kalimah'—laa ilaha illal-Aallah.]

The son of Mas^ud narrated that "**<God> will remove the Qur'an from between your backs in one night"** *[La younza^an-nal qur'anu min bayni aDh-hurikum—youssrah ^aleyhi laylan]*

The son of Mas^ud said, **"<God> will extract the Qur'an from the chests of people, and nothing of it will remain on Earth."** *[yadh-habu min ajwafil-rijal fala yabqah minhu shay'oon]*

Ibn Mas^ud said, **"Visit the Kaabah a lot more before it is lifted (to the Sky), and people forget its location. And increase your recitation of the Qur'an before it is raised <to the Sky>."** *[akthiru min ziyaarati hadhal bayt (i.e., kaabah) min qabli ay-yurfa^ wa yansan-nassu makanah. Wa akthiru min tilawatil qur'an min qabli ay-yurfa^.]*

They asked, **'O the father of ^Abdur-Rahman, the copies of the Qur'an will be raised, but how will its verses be removed from the chest of men?** [*Qalu ya aba ^Abdir-Rahman, hadhihil masahifu turfa^ fa kayfa ma-fi suduri-rijal?]*

Ibn Mas^ud replied, **"They will wake up and say, '*We used to talk about words and say certain words,*' and the people will return to the speech of ignorance and the sayings of ignorance, and that's how they will lose the knowledge <of knowing the Qur'an>."** *[Qala, yusbihuna wa yaquluna kunna natakallam bi kalamin wa naqulu qawlah wa yarji^un-nasu ila qawlil jahiliyyah wa ila hadeethil jahiliyya wa dhalika hina yaqa^ul qawlu ^aleyhim.]*

Chapter 11

Major Sign No.10

Slow-Moving Fire

The Major signs will pass by one by one. Are you with me? Is anyone awake? *What have you prepared for that Day? Are you ready for the Day of your inevitable departure?* Even if one lives a century or longer, the years are still very short compared to forever in the Afterlife. In the last 100 years, no worshipper of God will be left on Earth. Only the evil and most wicked people will remain alive. The Prophet, peace be upon him, likened these evil people who are quick with agility, like a bird, in their quickness to commit wicked evil deeds.

> Prophet Muhammad, peace be upon him, said, **"The people's wickedness will remain [*Khiffat at-Tayri] like the agility of a flying bird and [*Ahlam As-siba^] the dream of every fanged beast."**

This Hadith means these evil people will be quick to do wicked actions to satisfy their desires through any means possible. Similar in quickness to the speed and agility of a flying bird. **"People will be widespread enemies to one**

another, committing injustices and harming one another like the wild beasts attack their prey."

> Our Prophet, peace be upon him, described the state of wickedness of non-believers in the last one hundred years on Earth by saying, **"Those people will not acknowledge what is 'Good' <, i.e., what is rewardable> and will not reject what is 'wrong' <, i.e., what is sinful>. So, the devil will present himself to them at the time and say, "And don't you answer?" They will respond to their beloved Satan. "What is it you want us to do?" Satan will order them to worship idols so that they will comply and worship idols."**

This means these evil people will be quick to do evil actions to satisfy their desires through any means possible. Similar in quickness to the speed and agility of a flying bird. **"People will be widespread enemies to one another, committing injustices and harming one another like the wild beasts attacks its prey."**

> Lady ˆAisha said the Prophet, peace be upon him, said, **"The night and day will not cease to exist until the idols of Al-Laat and ˆUzza are worshipped <again>."**

This means that at the end of times when almost all Major Signs have happened, the remaining evil people on Earth will all be idol worshipers—following the blasphemous religion of their forefathers.

What Happens to the Blessed City of Medina?

As for the city of Medina, that's the very last Muslim stronghold. The last town to be deserted and ruined is this blessed city. The very blessed City of Medina is the final Muslim city to be in ruins on Earth. Afterward, the dogs or wolves will inhabit it.

At the end of time, Allah will send a wind or a breeze. This wind will come from under the remaining Muslims' armpits and take their souls. Every last of the believers will die and not one of them will remain. Only the very ignorant blasphemers will remain inhabiting the Earth. God will raise the Quran.

The disbelievers will not know Salah i.e. physical prayer. They will not be familiar with nor give any charity. They will live on Earth filled with enmity for one another for 100 years until Angel Isra'feel blows the Horn.

The blowing of the Horn will make the hearts of the idol worshippers physically burst in their chests. Those who were already deceased will become unconscious. The fate of humans, genies, and animals is death. Even angels will die and fall from the sky.

> **"As long as this nation, i.e., Followers of Prophet Muhammad are on Earth, belief will remain in Al-Madinah. Pious people will live in Al-Madinah," as our Prophet told us. Prophet Muhammad, peace be upon him, said, "There is great merit in the land of Ash-Sham. Angels cover these countries with their wings."** This Hadith signifies Islam will persevere in Madinah even during hardships until the last century on Earth.

The Prophet peace be upon him said, "Dogs (or Wolves) will attack it and chew on some of the Mosque's articles or the Pulpit." It is challenging to envision a time when only dogs or wolves will inhabit the Prophet's Mosque instead of worshipers. Allahu Akbar!

> The Prophet, peace be upon him, stated in the Hadith that **"Eman (Proper Belief in God) will one day be confined to the Blessed City of Medina as the snake is confined normally to its hole."**

In the last 100 years on Earth, when Medina is empty of believers, wild dogs or wolves will dwell in the Baqeeˆ graveyard, visited by billions of Muslims and houses the best of this Muslim Nation. Certainly, Medina has a better status than other places in the past and the future.

What Happens to the Ka^bah?

At the end of time, the City of Al-Madina shall be the last Islamic town to fall into ruin. As for the Ka^bah before Judgment Day, Mecca will be deserted before the end of the world. It will be destroyed by a blasphemer King, as mentioned in the Hadith, that he's an Abyssinian or Ethiopian. He will destroy the Ka^bah, searching for a treasure beneath it, and take the Ka^bah apart block by block.

> ^Abdullah the son of ^Amr said the Prophet, peace be upon him said, **"Dhul-Suwayqatayn from Abyssinia will ruin the Ka^bah and seize its buried treasures and kiswah,"** With his spade and pitch-axe, he will attack the Ka^bah, pick apart all its stones from the rubble, and take all its treasures until not a single soul on Earth remembers its location.

Major Sign No.10

The last of the Major signs will occur, a slow-moving fire of lava indicating the Day of Judgment is the nearest. A massive volcanic eruption will happen in the inner valley of ^Aden in Yemen, from 'The Sea of Hadramawt,' and will be the very last of the Major Signs that Judgment Day is so near!

> Hudhayfah Ibn Usayd said he heard the Prophet, peace be upon him, said what means, **"The last of them (i.e., the Major Signs) will be a great fire that shall start in ˆAden (Al-Yemen) in Hadramawt. And this fire spreads slowly and stays with the people, regardless of how much they try to avoid it. This vast fire will follow them if they travel down or up into other areas. Entirely unavoidable. They cannot extinguish it. This fire will be so great that it drives the people to the west, to the area of their Assembly."** ~ Narrated by Muslim

The Day of Resurrection will be on the land of Levant. The fire will spread slowly, not fast like the wind. People will attempt to escape this fire by moving westward – i.e., west of the Arabian Peninsula. As it progresses, driving and forcing the people from all countries to keep moving and scurrying to avoid its harm. Until all the remaining idol worshipers reach the land of Resurrection and Assembly—the land of the Levant countries—i.e., Syria, Lebanon, Palestine, and Jordan

Apocalypse: The Destruction of the Earth

God predestined the destruction of the Earth. This frightening event will occur during the stages of Judgment Day after Resurrection. There are 50 stages, and some consist of the various destructions of the Earth for the blasphemers to experience. The last of the evil and arrogant human blasphemers alive on Earth will experience the most severe torture of hearing the blast of the Horn.

God Revealed in the Qur'an an Ayah that means, <<The Day when the earthquake horn blast that is blown>>

After all 10 Major Signs occur, Angel Israfeel will blow the Horn very strongly for the first time, producing a frightening sound. The first person to hear the blow will be someone fixing the basin for their camels to drink. The blast's strength will cause the non-believers' hearts to rupture, and all remaining human beings will perish. All the living jinn will also die. All those who had already died will faint, except the souls of the martyrs already in Paradise.

Concerning Prophet Moses, Prophet Muhammad, peace be upon them, told us when God gave the mountain the power to see God, the mountain completely crumbled. When Moses saw the mountain crumble, he fainted already. Therefore, Prophet Muhammad, peace be upon him, said he did not know whether Moses would faint (again) when the Horn was blown the first time.

What will happen?

That blast shatters the skies and Earth and will remain broken and destroyed for 40 years. No one will be alive but Allah, the

Exalted Creator. Then Allah will resurrect Angel Israfeel back to life to stand up and blow his Horn again.

> God Revealed in the Qur'an in an Ayah that means, << **That's when the people come out of their grave and the hearts of the people on that Day will be pounding in fear. Their visions will be humbled. It is but a mere single blast (Second) of the Horn. And behold, they shall be standing upon the face of the Earth.>>**

Among the various events that will occur on the Day of Destruction:

- God will unite all the bodies of oceans all over the Earth and set them ablaze until they evaporate entirely.
- God will create the seven solid skies, each 500 years in thickness, to be folded like scrolls.
- All the mountains will crumble and become dust above the heads of the people.
- The stars will fall from space.
- The sun and moon will join and lose their light.
- And God knows all other events...

God revealed in the Holy Qur'an in Surat Al-Hajj verse 2 that means, << <On the Day of the Earth's Destruction> **The Day when every nursing mother will abandon who she is nursing** <out of severe fear>, **and every pregnant woman will give birth** <prematurely from terror>. **And you will see people** <as if they were> **drunk, although they will not be drunk; but the torture of Allah is** <extremely> **severe.** >>

Allah revealed in Surat Al-Qiyyamah verses 9–12, which means, <<**And the sun and the moon will join <They will rise from the west and lose their light>, on the Day one will cry, 'Where is the escape?' But no! There will be no refuge. All is <known> by your Lord on that Day.**>>

The Final Event Terminates All Life on Earth

One Day when the evil disbelievers least expect it, all of a sudden, Angel Israfeel, peace be upon him, will blow his Horn—the first blow. Since God created him, this honorable Angel has been awaiting Allah's order to blow this Horn.

When the order comes, this Angel will blow this Horn, and the tremendous blast will terrorize and frighten the disbelievers to the extent their heartstrings physically break, killing all remaining Humans, Jinn, and animals on Earth. At this time, Satan, the cursed, will also die.

All the Muslims who died before that time will lose consciousness except for the spirits of the martyrs in Paradise. For those who died before, their bodies already decayed, and their souls will lose consciousness. However, the bodies with souls remaining in them will experience a shock—even the Prophets will experience this shock without any pain.

The martyrs already in Paradise will not lose consciousness because Allah specified them with this specialness to inspire Muslims on Earth to pursue martyrdom. Although the Prophets are the highest in rank, much higher than martyrs, they will be shocked into unconsciousness but without pain.

> The Messenger of Allah, peace be upon him, mentioned in a Hadith, which Al-Bukhariyy related that means, **"Once the people get that shock on the Day of Judgment, I <Prophet Muhammad> will be the first one to wake up from it; I will then see Prophet Moses (Musa) holding onto the leg of the Throne <The ˆArsh which is the ceiling of Paradise>. I will not know whether Prophet Moses woke up before me or was spared from it because he had already experienced the shock at Mount Tur before."**

Almost all the angels will die after the death of all the humans. The last of the Angels to die will be the Angel of Death—the Honorable Angel ˆAzra’eel.

Some scholars said about who will be exempt from dying after the first blow of the Horn, **“Except the angels in charge of Paradise, angels in charge of Hellfire, angels that carry the Throne, Al-Hoor, Al-Wildan, and the snakes and scorpions of hellfire.”** After Angel Israfeel blows the Horn the first time, this Angel, along with most of the angels, will die too.

Forty years later, God created Angel Israfeel to return to life, so this Angel will stand up again and blow the Horn a second time—signaling the commencement of Judgment Day.

The first stage of Judgment Day is the Resurrection of all the dead people and jinn who ever lived—from the time of Prophet Adam until the very end of life on Earth.

Angels will guide the masses for the stages of **‘Questioning’ (as-Su’al) and ‘Judgment’ (Al-Hisab).**

Every animal and insect that ever possessed a spirit, lived, walked, or crawled on this Earth will resurrect, too. On that Day, God will create a day of Justice for all the animals harmed because of their physical disabilities.

After this event of Justice, God will create all the animals and insects to turn into dust (soil) since they never disobeyed God while living on Earth. There is no Paradise or Hellfire for animals in the Hereafter because they lived their life in a status of not being accountable.

This is the Day of Tremendous Fear.

Judgment Day: The Day of Greatest Fear!

We will be most concerned with ourselves on that Great Day, and most of humanity (not all) will assemble in the described appearance.

> God revealed in Surat ˆAbasa verses 33—37 what means, **<<Then, when the Deafening <Frightening second> Blast <of the Horn> comes to pass (signaling the beginning of Judgment Day)—on that Day every person will flee from their siblings and <even> their mother and father, and <even> their spouse and children. Everyone will only be concerned about their own <safety>.>>**

The Prophet said, **"Most humans will assemble after resurrection from their graves—barefoot, naked, and uncircumcised."** Of course, that is **not** how the Prophets and Righteous Muslims assemble, but most people are as mentioned.

Lady ˆAisha asked, **"O Messenger of Allah, won't the people be looking at each other's unlawful nakedness?"**

The Prophet, peace be upon him, answered, **"The situation will be much greater than to care about that."**

Where is the escape from that Day? *There is no escape.*

> God revealed in Surat Ar-Rahman, verse 33 that means, <<**O assembly of Jinn and Humans! If you can penetrate beyond the realm of the heavens and the Earth, then do so. <But> you cannot do that without <God's> Authority.** >>
>
> God revealed in the Holy Qur'an Surah Al-Qamar, verse 7, which means, <<**With eyes downcast, they (people) will resurrect from the graves as if they were swarming Locusts.** >>

God assembles the People on Judgment Day after He creates their Resurrection from their graves, and they will be so numerous that they will appear like locusts.

Judgment Day is so Near...

Brothers and Sisters, do you have good deeds that you are hopeful of God's acceptance on that Grand Day? Have you learned the obligatory religious knowledge of Islam? Have you taught others the obligatory Islamic religious knowledge?

Muhammad, our Prophet, peace be upon him; the best creations experienced death. Do you think you will stay alive

without dying?? By Allah, certainly not. Judgment for all people is so much closer, and most people are unconscious and oblivious of what awaits them.

Do you want Everlasting Pleasure? Or do you want Everlasting Torture?

The one who obeys Allah crying, Allah enters him into Paradise while he is laughing. By Allah, God did not create us to play, have fun and make money. Our existence on this Earth is short-term, and no one remains in this worldly life. The path to Paradise is not an effortless road—it is a road filled with calamities, whereas seeking worldly pleasures and desires is the path to hellfire. You ultimately want the everlasting abode of Paradise. So, pull up your sleeves and prepare for serious work towards achieving Paradise!

> Imagine that you are fortunate to be among the dwellers in the Hereafter, who will hear the Angel's call saying, **"O Dwellers of Paradise, for you everlasting life without ever dying. O Dwellers of Paradise, for you everlasting youth without ever getting old, for you everlasting health without sickness. For you everlasting happiness without ever experiencing worry."**

O Allah, I ask you that we will be among those whom the Angel will tell these beautiful words.

O Allah, we ask you for Paradise and all the sayings and actions that bring us closer to Paradise, and we seek refuge with you from the devil to protect us from all the expressions, words, phrases, and actions of the Dwellers of Hellfire.

O Allah, grant us patience in this Earthly world and remember your Afterlife...

Chapter 12

The Day of Resurrection in Detail

50 Stations; 1000 Years Each

Each body decays until only a tiny piece of the spine remains, called the coccyx bone, which is as small as a mustard seed. Under no circumstances will this little bone decompose. The coccyx will remain intact regardless of whether the body was cremated, crushed, or eaten by animals.

God revealed that a viscose rain resembling the thickness of semen would fall from the sky on that Day. It will fall in sparse drops and regenerate around its coccyx bone, causing each body to grow back, like a plan. Every human body starts to re-emerge from the coccyx bone, resulting in mass recreation.

In *Bukhariyy's* *Sahih* and *At-Tirmidhiyy'sSunan*, the Prophet said, peace be upon him, **"The people on the Judgment Day will be gathered as first created, without shoes and clothes and uncircumcised. However, some people, like the Prophets, will not be naked."**

Every person will have the same body part God gave them at birth.

> The Prophet, peace be upon him, recited a verse in Surat Yaseen that means, **<<Just as God created the people at the beginning, God will recreate them.>>** This is what God revealed, and it will happen.

You will come back to life as you were before your death. Upon revival, you will be fully restored to your original form, including any lost limbs or body parts you may have had in your earthly life. After being restored, each decomposed body reunites with its soul. Even after decomposing, God creates each person's resurrection. For the bodies that did not decompose, God reunites their soul with it and revives each person with the same body he and she had in this life.

Resurrection:

> **God revealed an Ayah that means, <<The Day when the horn is blown, and you shall come forth in crowds.>>**

This verse mentions that Angel Israfeel will blow the horn a second time when all the humans will resurrect from their graves. Prophet Mohammed will be the first to rise from his grave; peace be upon him. When he comes out, he will see that Prophet Moses is already holding onto one of the pillars of the ˆArsh (the Throne).

After the Meccans, the people of Medina will resurrect next, and then the people of Al-Taa'if will exit their tombs. Then, the rest of the Humanity will rise from their graves.

<<You have been recreated and brought back to life for Our judgment, just as <God> created you the first time.>>, i.e., Naked, barefoot, and uncircumcised.

The Prophet said peace be upon him, **"Most humans will assemble after resurrection from their graves—barefoot, naked, and uncircumcised."** Of course, that is not how the Prophets and Righteous Muslims assemble, but most people are as mentioned.

Lady ˆAisha asked, **"O Messenger of Allah, won't the people be looking at each other's unlawful nakedness?"** The Prophet, peace be upon him, answered, **"No, the situation is too serious for that."**

When Judgment Day comes, for most people, only self-preservation will matter. People will not be concerned that you are naked or about you. No one will care about race either, if he is black, or you are black, or if you are Arab, or if he is Arab. Race will be of no concern to anyone on that Day.

None of the Prophets will be naked on Judgment Day, although they will receive unique clothing. Prophet Abraham will be the first to wear this unique clothing; peace be upon him.

<<The Day when a person would flee from his brother (his closest of kin), his mother and father, and his wife and children. For every one of them, there is an affair that concerns him.>>

This Ayah means there will come a day when people don't care about you because Judgment Day's torture is too severe. Only those who befriended and loved one another for Allah's sake will remain friends in the Hereafter. Otherwise, all counterfeit love of this world will turn into enmity come Judgment Day.

<<On that Day, had you seen it? Every nursing woman. If there were a nursing woman on that Day, she would abandon her baby. Had there been a pregnant woman, they would have had a miscarriage. And you would see the people as if they were drunk. But they are not drunk. Rather, it is the torture of Allah that is very severe.>>

Who will be clothed on judgment day while everyone else is naked? Those who earned halal money.

Who will satiated and satisfied while everyone else is starving on the Day of Resurrection? The individuals who consumed halal.

Who will ride on Judgment Day while everyone else stands? Those who woke up to pray at night during their lifetime.

<<A fitting compensation.>> Your deeds determine the reward or punishment that Allah will give you.

<<And every self shall come forth, will come out of its grave, and it shall find two angels, one named Sa'iq and the other named Shaheed.>>

Two pairs of angels, ***Sa'iq and Shaheed,*** stand guard, preventing anyone from escaping. God, the Exalted, will bring back to life absolutely every human that ever existed to the place of the assembly called *'Al-MaHshar.'* God will resurrect and gather every living creature that ever lived among the humans, genies, and animals from the time of Prophet Adam, peace be upon him until Angel Israfeel blows the horn. All of them will be gathered in one place.

<<On the Day when Allah gathers them all (Humans and Jinns. O ye assemblage of genies, Oh you genies, you have done much to humanity. A person will be resurrected on Judgment Day, and he will see his associate Devil. When he encounters and meets his Qareen, He will see the one who was invisible to him all this time in his world. He would say, "Woe is me. Had only there been between you and me the distance between the east and the west." >>

The herding of people will make the place of assembly incredibly crowded. Everyone will be moved to a dark area near the Bridge (As-Siraat), and meanwhile, Allah creates the flattening of the Earth, leveling the mountains that will blow away like tiny pieces of cotton.

<<And the Earth will be flat. And Allah, the Exalted, will expand the Earth. <Allah, the Exalted> will stretch out and expand the Earth and then bring back the people from the darkness to the now-changed Earth to experience Judgment Day. When the sunlight is extinguished, when the stars dim, when the mountains move from their places, and when the beasts are herded (the animals will resurrect on Judgment Day, and then they will pay each other back.) >>

God will create horns for the hornless sheep that were attacked by horned sheep so that they can fight back on Judgment Day before both turn into soil.

<<And when the oceans/seas are set ablaze, and when the selves are paired (matched) >>

There are various interpretations from trustworthy scholars about the meaning of this verse. Some said it means "*The reunion of the bodies and souls." Some said, "The spouses reunion will occur on Judgment Day." And others said, "When the good/righteous come together versus when the wicked/evil come together."*

<<And when the sky is ripped away and torn, Judgment Day is—Yamun FaSL—' The Day of Segregation.' >>

Each nation will have unity, and believers will be united separately from blasphemers. The various nations of each Prophet who followed Islam will unite. The different blasphemer nations will unite, such as Christians, Jews, and followers of other religions.

<<Some will approach others wondering and say, 'You used to have authority. Is there anything you can do?' So those leaders will say to their followers, 'You are responsible for yourselves. You are the ones who chose not to believe.' And we had no authority over you to make you believe in blasphemy. We couldn't force you to believe in blasphemy. You were transgressing people and accountable for yourselves. And now the revelation of our Lord, which is His Promise to torture us, has come true. Indeed, we shall all taste the tortures. So, yes, we misguided you. We were misguided. >>

On Judgment Day, the believers will stand in 120 rows—two-thirds of those rows (80 lines) are the Muslim Nation and followers of Prophet Muhammad; peace be upon him. Only one-third of Muslims going to Paradise will be for all other prophets, from the time of Prophet Adam until Prophet Jesus, peace be upon them all. As for the blasphemers, they are vastly, much, much more because most human beings will be in Hellfire.

The Questioning (Al-Hisab):

The Day of Judgment is a very long day that lasts for 50,000 years. It consists of 50 stations, each with a duration of 1,000 years. However, the pious Muslims will be spared from anguish; therefore, they will not feel the long timeline like everyone else. Instead, the pious Muslim will feel the time pass as if he is waiting for one afternoon prayer.

<<And indeed, they are all sharing in the torture on that Day. A Day whose duration is 50,000 years.>>

Fifty thousand years is the timeline for sending humans and jinn to their earned everlasting residences - either in blissful Heaven or inmates of the inferno forever.

The First Station: Answering 4 Questions

God questions all the people and genies about their deeds, enabling every person who is the slave of God to hear God's Eternal Speech. All people and genies will understand that God is questioning them about what they did and how they used the endowments God gave them in this life.

The pious believer will feel delighted being questioned, while the blasphemers will be so devastated that they would have perished from their anguish at this stage if they could die. However, death will be extinct in the Hereafter.

Ahmad and *At-Tirmidhiyy*, narrated that the Prophet said, peace be upon him, **"Everyone among you will hear the <Eternal> Speech of God on Judgment Day without needing anyone to interpret the meaning of God's Speech."**

This Hadith means that everyone will understand God's questioning, which does not take long.

The Qur'an proves in **Surat-al-Anˆam, verse 62, and Surat-al Baqarah, verse 202** that God's Speech is not composed of sounds, letters, or language as in human speech. If it were, questioning everyone would have taken a very long time. This stage of Judgment Day alone would have taken over 50,000 years because each person who existed performed countless deeds in their lifetime.

Some creations have an incredibly long lifespan, like Satan, the devil. He is an example of a super long-living creature and will finally die with the very last batch of humans on Earth upon the blow of the horn. If God's speech were like human speech, Satan's exclusive questioning about all his evil deeds would have been an extremely long and time-consuming process.

However, God revealed in the Qur'an that His Questioning is very quick. Therefore, the Speech of God is dissimilar to the speech of the creations in every aspect, as evidenced by the following.

Prophet Muhammad, peace be upon him, conveyed the following Hadith that At-Tirmidhiyy narrated:

"When the people are first gathered on the Day of Judgment, after resurrection from their graves at the first stage and before a person can move a step, they will be questioned about four matters:

1. **What did you do with your knowledge?** *Did you acquire the obligatory religious knowledge, and did you implement it as ordered?*
2. **What did you do with your money, and how did you**

acquire it? *Was it acquired and spent in a lawful or unlawful manner?*

3. **What did you do with your body that you were given?** *Did you use your body to obey God by praying or to commit sins?*

4. **What did you do with your lifetime?** *Did you spend your time alive in a lawful manner, or did you waste your life committing sins?*

The Day Full Justice Prevails:

The Prophet, peace be upon him, said, **"The one who wronged his brother or sister, let him make restitution from injustice before it is too late. No one can clear themselves of injustice by using the dinar or dirham on Judgment Day."**

Muslim in As-Sahih and At-Tirmidhiyy in As-Sunan, narrated that the Prophet said, peace be upon him, **"Everyone would get his right on Judgment Day to the point that the sheep with horns butted a sheep without horns in this life, on Judgment Day, God will create horns for that sheep with which to butt."**

Because animals are not Islamically accountable and do not go to Paradise or Hellfire, they will all turn into dust after getting their justice on Judgment Day. Upon witnessing the animal's justice, the blasphemers will regret their human existence and say, **"I wish I turned to dust."** In other words, the blasphemers will wish they had lived on this Earth as animals, not human beings.

However, God eternally destined everlasting suffering without death for all the accountable blasphemers who will continue to suffer at every stage of Judgment Day until they reach the final abode of suffering—Hellfire forever and ever.

On that Grand Day, complete justice will prevail for the Muslim believers who chose to avoid injustice in this life because they trusted their Creator would grant their rights. For this reason, many righteous Muslims don't retaliate against their perpetrators when unfairly treated. They say, *"I leave that for Judgment Day"* because they firmly believe in the reality of what God revealed will happen on that Grand Day.

During Judgment Day, God will silence the mouths of blasphemers at one of the fifty stations, leaving them unable to speak. Instead of speaking voluntarily, their skin, hands, and legs will testify about their life's actions. **Even the ground will give testimony to the deeds performed upon it, as stated in the Quran in Surat-uz-Zalzalah.**

Our Prophet, peace be upon him, as narrated by *SunaAt-Tirmidhiyy* in *AsSunan*, recited verse 4 of *Surat-uz-Zalzalah, which means* **<<On that Day the Earth will tell its news.>>** The Prophet asked his Companions, **"Do you know the news?"** They said, *"God and His Messenger know best.*

The Prophet said, peace be upon him, **"On that Day, the Earth will bear witness to the people's actions on it. The spot where the person disobeyed God will speak on Judgment Day and say, 'Such a person did such-and-such a thing on this**

day.' Disclosing the good deeds, the Earth will say, 'So and so did such-and-such good thing on that day.' This is the news of the Earth."

HISAB Has More Than 1 Meaning:

Lady ^A'ishah reported that the Prophet, peace be upon him, said, **"The person questioned extensively on Judgment Day will be a loser and tortured."**

'HISAB' in this Hadith *means* ***'Severe Questioning'*** *about everything in the book—it is reserved only for those who will receive punishment.*

Lady ^A'ishah recited a verse to the Prophet, which means, **<<The person who receives his book <of deeds> with his right hand will be questioned lightly.>>**

'HISAB' in this verse *means* ***'The Presenting of the Deeds'*** *and not 'Severe Questioning.'*

The Prophet, peace be upon him, replied, **"That is only the presentation of the deeds. The one whom Allah does not will torture, will not be questioned about every deed he did."** ~ Narrated by At-Tirmidhiyy.

On Judgment Day, the questioning of the Prophets will be to show their great merit rather than to reprimand them since their book of deeds is entirely free of sins. **No one Prophet ever committed blasphemy, enormous sins, or small abject sins that show a low character.**

The only sin that is mentally possible to occur from a Prophet is a small, non-abject sin that does not show low character. If a Prophet commits a small, non-abject sin, he is immediately guided to repent and will be forgiven.

An example of this type of sin *is when Adam ate from a tree that Allah ordered him to avoid and when Prophet Jonas left his disbelieving nation without God revealing for him to go.*

Repentance is Obligatory:

God obligated every human and genie to become Muslim and obey God, but Allah did not Eternally Will that everyone on Earth would do so. This obligation upon Humanity and genies remains active despite most of Humanity's disobedience.

God obligates the believer who disobeys God by sinning to repent immediately. Since a person doesn't know when their death is destined, repenting promptly from sins is the smartest choice if safety in the Hereafter is your goal.

> ***No one other than God erases sins. Only Allah, the Creator, is the One who erases sins; No creation erases sins.***

On Judgment Day, from His generosity, God will conceal and not expose some of the enormous Muslim sinners who die without repenting. However, many Muslim sinners and all the blasphemers will be exposed on Judgment Day. However, for everyone who repents of their sins before death, God will erase their sins.

One of the tortures on Judgment Day is humiliation. An angel will publicly reveal the sins of blasphemers and some believers who died without repenting from their enormous sins.

Book of Deeds:

The day of reckoning will arrive, and every accountable person, regardless of religion, will receive their recorded book of deeds from the angels. Joyfully, the Muslim believer will take his book of deeds with his right hand. All the accountable disbelievers will receive their book of deeds in shame, with their left hand behind their back. The appearance of their books will bring happiness to the believers while causing tremendous grief to the disbelievers.

<<And the book of deeds shall be placed <in their left hand>, and you will see the criminals <blasphemers> afraid of what is in it. >>

Allah, the Creator of the Universe, named the disbelievers *Criminals.*

<<And they will say, 'Whoa. What is wrong with this book? This book misses nothing big or small.' And they will find all that they have done present and documented. >>

<<And your Lord does not wrong anyone. As for the one given his book <of deeds> **in his right hand, then he shall**

experience an easy presentation of his deeds. His Hisab <means his deeds presented to him> will be easy, meaning the one whose HISAB is easy. He will experience an easy presentation of his deeds and will not be questioned about everything he did. And he will turn to his family happy in the afterlife. He will say come and read my book.>>

That's because the believer is delighted and a winner on that day.

<<They (believers) **fulfilled their vows. They fulfilled their obligations. They honored their promises. And they feared a day whose calamity and hardship are widespread. And they give food despite their desire for it. They give charities although they want to keep those charities and monies for themselves. And they feed the orphans. They even feed the non-Muslim prisoner and treat him well. >>**

<<We are feeding you solely for the sake of Allah," say those who believe. "We do not want from you any reward. We do not want from you any thanks. We fear a day from our Lord that looks grim, and its eyebrows furrowed" (describing the day).>>

<<So Allah will protect them from the evils of that day and give them the brightness of beauty and blissful joy. The believer says, "I was certain I would be accountable for my actions and face judgment. I learned it in this life and firmly believe in it.">>

The believer has absolute Faith that Judgment Day is for sure.

<<And as for the blasphemer who receives his book of deeds behind his back with his left hand. He will say, "Whoa, to me. I wish this book were never given to me." The one who gets his book behind his back, his right hand will be chained to his neck. He will call out for his destruction and will burn in the inferno. >>

<<In this lifetime with his family, he is happy. He used to think that he would not come back. Indeed, he will come back, and his Lord knew all about him. >>

Some people will be so happy, while most will feel the worst grief.

> *Anyone who misrepresents the Qur'an and believes contrary to its teachings is not a Muslim, even if he is a person of perceived status – like a memorizer of the Qur'an or the lead shaykh in the Haram Mosque or his name is Muhammad or ˆAbdur-RaHman or they have millions of followers on social media or millions or billions of dollars.*

Such people, even if they perform Islamic rituals like Salat, Fasting, and Recitation of the Qur'an with invalid blasphemous belief in Allah, will yield zero rewards, no matter how many years they perform those rituals.

Blasphemers with Invalid Belief Have NO Good Deeds

For example, there are individuals in our world called Wahhabis who dress and speak like they belong to the Muslim community. This group identifies as Muslim; although they are not the majority Muslims, they consist of several million. Sadly, their creed similar to Paganism, contradicts and belies the Qur'an and Hadith by falsely claiming God resembles the creations when the Qur'an explicitly revealed that **<<*Nothing is like Allah in any way whatsoever.*>>**

God rewards or punishes people in the Hereafter based on their obedience to His orders in this life. **The Blasphemers' Book of Deeds contains only their sins** and is void of good deeds. In contrast, the believer will see all the good and bad deeds in their book.

<<Rather, on Judgment Day, those people, their good deeds will be like dust on a windy day>>

This Ayah compares the good deeds of blasphemers to dust on a windy day. When the gusty wind blows, the pile of dust will vanish without any sign of it ever being there. That is what happens to all the blasphemers' earthly good deeds – they disappear!

A Believer's Book of Deeds has *three* entry types - *fulfilled obligations, recommended good deeds, and sins committed without repentance.* The' Permissible' deeds are ***deleted*** from everyone's books because such actions as eating lentils instead of chickpeas or drinking tea instead of juice do not have any merit for reward. Sadly, most people spend their entire earthly lives fulfilling their desires in this unrewardable category.

The Messenger of Allah said, peace be upon him, **"Whoever God excessively questions will receive torture."** This Hadith means that anyone God questions about every evil action they ever committed will be tortured.

The Messenger of Allah, peace be upon him, said, **"There is none of you but his Lord speaks to him on the Day of Resurrection. And there will be no interpreter to explain the Speech of God to him. Allah is the quickest questioner."** God's Eternal and Everlasting Speech is not a language, words, or letters and does not take time.

In the Hereafter, to be questioned means Allah, the Exalted, will question in accountability His slaves by making every person, believer, and nonbeliever hear God's uncreated and unimaginable Speech. More than trillions of creatures will hear Allah's Speech, and that number is only known to God.

They will all hear the uncreated Speech of God that is not a sound, letter, or language, and everyone understands something different. Each person will realize they are being questioned about their entire life specifically.

When the pious believer hears the Speech of Allah, he would die of happiness if he could. Upon hearing the Speech of

God, the Blasphemer would die of despair, sadness, and dismay if he could.

No Death in the Afterlife:

On Judgment Day, God creates death in the appearance of a lamb between Paradise and Hellfire, and an honorable angel will slaughter it to signify to the dwellers of Paradise and Hellfire that the Afterlife has no end, only everlasting life.

The Blasphemer will swear he believed in Allah, but everyone will testify against him. He replies, "**No witness will suffice for me except myself.**" Then Allah, the Exalted, will seal his mouth and make his skin, hands, and feet speak for him.

Surat Yaseen, Verse 65 means, <<On this Day, we shall seal their mouths, and then their hands shall speak to Us. And their feet shall testify about the deeds they used to commit.>>

<< And then that person's body parts will tell on him. Then Allah will enable him to speak again, and he will say to his body parts, 'What's wrong with you?' And they (i.e., body parts) would say, "Allah, the one who made speaking things speak, enabled us to speak." >>

<<And even the ground will testify on that Day. On that Day, the Earth will tell its news. >> *May Allah protect us.*

In the places where the person disobeyed God, the ground will say, ***"He was upon me here when he did this and that."*** And likewise, whoever did good, the Earth will bear witness. Allah will make the Earth alive without giving it a soul, although it will have knowledge and understanding. Allah will enable the ground to speak, and it will testify to support you or against you. May Allah protect us.

Prophets are also Questioned:

Prophets are questioned not for reprimand or punishment but to highlight their tremendous merit.

> God revealed in Surat Al-Ma'idah verse 116 that means, <<**And** <on Judgment Day> **when Allah says, 'O Jesus, son of Mary, is it true that you said to the people, take me and my mother both as gods besides God?' (Jesus) He says, 'Glory is yours, O Allah. I would not say what I have no right to say. If I said that, O Allah, then you know I said it. You know what, all that hides inside me. Indeed, You** <alone> **are the Knower of all the unseen.'**>>

The Scale/Balance (Al-Mizan):

On Judgment Day, there will be a Balance, a real instrument like the scale in this life with two pans connected to a bar and the fulcrum.

One pan is for the good deeds, and the other is for the evil deeds.

Each person's deeds are weighed in this Balance, which is vast and much more extensive than any scale we have seen in this life.

Some scholars interpreted the texts to mean, 'On that Day, God will create the deeds to become objects that will be placed in the pans.' Other scholars interpret the Book of Deeds written by the two angels as what is weighed. Regardless of how the deeds are weighed, the human deeds will be weighed on an absolute scale.

God revealed in the *Qur'an* that the weighing on Judgment Day is very accurate and just.

- *Will the pages or Book of Deeds be weighed?*
- *Will the Deeds be transformed, taking shape as bodies and put into these pans to be Weighed?*
- *Could people themselves be Weighed? Allah knows everything.*

Gabriel (Jibreel) and Michael (Mika'eel) are two special angels who will manage the weighing of the deeds, good and bad, on Judgment Day.

Those who have *more good deeds* on the scale will be *safe.*

People with the *same amount of good and bad deeds* have a lower rank than the believers with more good deeds; however, they are also *safe*. Those with an equal balance of good and bad deeds hold a higher status than those with evil deeds that surpass their good deeds.

The believers with more evil deeds than good deserve punishment, and only those believers that God forgives will be safe from torture.

If a believer's good deeds outweigh their bad, God will admit them into Heaven without torture.

If believers have more bad deeds than good, they may go to Hellfire before entering Paradise. Whether God punishes this sinner Muslim first or forgives them without torture is under God's will.

Also, all accountable blasphemers will have more bad deeds because they will have no good deeds. For sure, God will punish them in Hellfire.

Pre-Requisite for the Acceptance of Good Deed:

Faith is a pre-requisite necessity for any good deeds to be accepted. Therefore, blasphemers will not have good deeds in the Hereafter, only sins. The sin of blasphemy has no other consequence than punishment in Hellfire.

When a believer's evil deeds outweigh their good, they are subject to Allah's Will. What Allah eternally willed and destined to happen for such people will occur. God will either punish or forgive that person. The Muslim sinners Allah

Eternally willed to grant forgiveness on Judgment Day will receive forgiveness.

The Muslims, with Good Deeds exceeding their Bad, will enter Paradise without torture and <u>not need</u> intercession from any creation.

Those with Equal Amounts of Good and Bad Deeds are Muslims, who will be *safe* but not among the first to enter Paradise. These believers must wait outside the wide wall encircling Paradise until the first group of devout Muslims enters before they are granted access to Paradise afterward.

Sinner Muslims who died without repenting from their enormous sins will have their evil deeds outweigh their good deeds and deserve God's torture. They are at risk of being tortured in Hellfire without God's forgiveness.

Some sinner Muslims will receive mercy due to someone making intercession for them, resulting in getting out of Hellfire earlier.

Some sinful Muslims will not receive intercession and face harsh punishment in Hellfire. Any amount of time spent in Hellfire is severe punishment.

The Holy Qur'an confirms that some sinner Muslims will enter Hellfire and suffer therein before entering Paradise. Muslims must beware of those who believe the Qur'an. It is blasphemy for a person to say or request forgiveness for ALL Muslims, as it contradicts and belies verses in the Qur'an that explicitly state some Muslims will be punished in Hellfire. As confirmed by the Holy Qur'an, Sinner Muslims who die as true believers who enter Hellfire will not remain forever, even if they have committed a mountain of sins.

> Prophet Muhammad, peace be upon him, said, **"Some Muslims on Judgment Day will be 'Bankrupt.' These are the Muslims who performed good deeds sometimes and treated other Muslims unjustly. On Judgment Day, the Muslims he wronged will take from his good deeds. If he runs out of his own earned reward to give to those he wronged, the sinner Muslim will receive from the sins of the people he wronged, thereby increasing his sins. He will fall into Hellfire and be among the Muslims who will first suffer in Hellfire before entering Paradise."** ~ Narrated by Ibn Hibban and Muslim

The Prophet, peace be upon him, said that **on Judgment Day, a person will not remember any good deeds that he did. Then, the angels will bring a tablet with the Shahadatan, i.e., The Testifications of Faith, written on it and put it on his pan of good deeds.** This person benefited because he was a genuine Muslim who said and believed the Shahadatan. God will create this tablet alone to outweigh this Muslim's sinful deeds, although he is not pious. Of course, this does not happen for every Muslim because God confirmed in the Qur'an that some Sinner Muslims will surely be punished in Hellfire before going to Paradise.

The blasphemer will not have any good deeds in the pan of good deeds. *Why?*

Because God already compensated all the disbelievers in their earthly life for their good deeds. Even those who deny God's existence or worship other than God invalidly, God still provided for them many mercies and worldly pleasures. God rewarded and compensated the blasphemers for their good deeds with earthly blessings, like happiness, health, wealth, and children.

Other than Islamic icons and valid acts of worship to God, this earthly life is worthless to God.

For a person to be a winner and rewarded in the afterlife, a person must believe correctly in God in this life before death. He must not neglect **the first and most crucial Obligation upon them, i.e., To believe in God and His Messenger, Muhammad, peace be upon him.**

Nothing in this world is more valuable than believing in the creedal statement of Islam. It is the only KEY to enter PARADISE.

All the rewards granted by God come from His mercy. Nothing is obligatory for the Creator to do. God is not obligated to reward the obedient people either.

Once the Prophet, peace be upon him, said, **"No one's deeds admit him into Paradise."**

Someone asked the Prophet, *"Even you, O Messenger of God?"*

The Prophet, peace be upon him, answered, **"Even me, only if God endows His mercy upon me. Seek the correct path."**

God rewards and punishes based on generosity and justice. While God promised to reward believers, He doesn't need to. Nothing is mandatory for God to do, ever. If God punishes the obedient believers, this would not be injustice.

Because injustice is impossible to be attributed to God—injustice means the use of something without the right. Of course, Allah is the only Creator, and He owns absolutely everything.

The Bridge (As-Sirat):

One of the stages on Judgment Day is for the people to attempt to cross the Bridge. It is attached to the changed Earth on one side, and it travels upwards toward Paradise on the other side, exiting on spacious land outside the Gates of Paradise. The changed Earth is much lower than the level of Paradise, so the walk on the Bridge is hazardous.

The Prophet, peace be upon him, said "**The Bridge is thinner than a hair and sharper than a sword <a metaphor for how**

dangerous it is>, and crossing it depends on (the acceptance of) good deeds. The Prophet meant this figuratively, not literally. This Hadith shows the danger of the Bridge being treacherous on Judgment Day.

70,000 Angels using 70,000 chains will pull a segment (not all) of Hellfire and position it under the Bridge. Crossing the Bridge is difficult due to its steep slope, slippery surface, hooked sides, and the loud, raging sound of Hellfire below.

A person's safety while crossing this Bridge is 100% contingent upon the number of good deeds they have done in this life. Only God knows the precise amount of accepted good deeds any believer has accomplished.

> *Many people today have invalid beliefs and invalid worship. They may think they have performed many good deeds, but come to Judgment Day, they will have nothing but evil deeds.*

This stage on Judgment Day is one of the scariest and most dangerous because it is vast and slippery and stretches over a portion of Hellfire that all humans will traverse.

When a Prophet's nation of believers crosses the Bridge, the Prophet of that nation will pray to Allah for their safety. Some of those Muslims will cross that Bridge crawling across, while some will walk through, and others will run across it, although it's very slippery.

On this terrifying Bridge's edges will be hooks and claws that will gash many people passing, snagging them to throw into Hellfire. These hooks will drag some Muslim sinners until they come very close to falling off the Bridge. After experiencing scratches and fear from the claws, God will save some sinner Muslims from falling into Hellfire.

The speed of the people going over the Bridge is according to the acceptable good deeds they did in this life. The claws will pull some people off the Bridge, so they fall into Hell.

Some Muslims will be clawed off the Bridge, but as they fall, they will be hooked and clawed back onto the Bridge to continue crossing. This terrifying scare could happen many times as this sinner Muslim attempts to cross this Bridge and eventually be safe from entering Hellfire.

However, honorable Muslims won't even step physically onto this Bridge. Instead, they will fly over it as fast as a bolt of lightning or as fast as the blink of an eye.

For those who resurrect as disbelievers they have no hope of crossing this Bridge but fall immediately into Hellfire with their initial step.

Some Muslim enormous sinners will step on it and fall into Hellfire. In contrast, other Muslims' enormous sinners will eventually cross safely to the other end, narrowly escaping being engulfed in Hellfire.

Intercession (Shafa^ah):

Prophet Muhammad, peace be upon him, spoke of several stages of Judgment Day, when God will allow intercession for sinner Muslims. On Judgment Day, intercession is reserved only for Enormous Muslim Sinners. A pious Muslim does not need any mediation.

Definition: *Intercession is the asking of God to help and benefit someone else. This special asking is performed by some creations that God deemed to have merit, who will ask God to forgive or reduce the punishment of Muslim believers deserving of punishment.*

Muslims are of two types on Judgment Day:

1. **Muslims who are safe** and will **not be tortured** in Hellfire and
2. **Muslims who are unsafe** and will be **tortured** in Hellfire for a period.

Those Muslims who are ***'Unforgiven Enormous sinners*** will face torture and humiliation from Allah. God allows some of His creations to intercede for some sinner Muslims; however, anyone who died a blasphemer will never receive any intercession. When permitted, Muslim intercessors will request God to either decrease or end the punishment of some of the tortured Muslims.

On Judgment Day, intercession may happen during the sun's

torture and after crossing the Bridge. After the phase of crossing the Bridge, some Muslims would have fallen into Hellfire. Some Muslims who made it across the Bridge safely will ask God to relieve their fellow Muslims in Hellfire earlier than they deserve.

<<Those who neglected believing in and preparing for Judgment Day say, "Indeed, the Messengers of our Lord have come with the truth. So, are there any intercessors for us so that they could intercede for us? Or can we be returned to the earthly life to do deeds other than those we did? They have failed themselves. Those idols will be nowhere to be found, and no one will help them.>>

> God revealed in Surat-Al-Anbiya', verse 28, which means **<<The intercessors do not intercede except for those who died Muslim.>>**

> Prophet Muhammad, peace be upon him, said, **"My intercession is for the major sinners of my Nation,"** and **"The one who visited my grave will receive my intercession (if needed)."**

Who are the Intercessors Permitted to Intercede?

Intercession is permitted when God permits the high-ranking Muslims. The following intercessors can intercede by asking

Allah, the Exalted, to relieve some sinful Muslims from torture.

- ***All the Prophets for their followers,***
- ***Angels,***
- ***Practicing Muslims Scholars,***
- ***Martyrs of the battlefield will be allowed to intercede for 70 of their Muslim Sinner relatives,***
- ***Children who die before puberty can intercede for their Muslim parents (only), not their non-Muslim parents.***

The Torture of the Sun:

On Judgment Day, one of the fifty stages will be the sun descending very close to peoples' heads—only a mile or two away.

Many people will suffer in accordance with their sins as if they are melting under the sun and sweating profusely. For some individuals, their perspiration reaches their heels. In comparison, others will be drenched in sweat that comes to their knees.

Other peoples' sweat will reach their waists; for many, it will get to the middle of their ears. These people must raise their heads to avoid drowning in sweat that is self-contained within their bodies and separate from everyone else.

When the sun descends so close to the people, the only shade will be for pious and righteous Muslims, who will be protected underneath the shadow of the ceiling of Paradise, the largest creation. Shading the honorable Muslims only, the Ceiling of Paradise protects these honorable Muslims from the harm and heat of the excruciating sun on that grand day.

> *Be careful of misguided groups worldwide who mistranslate this Hadith and fall into blasphemy by falsely claiming the shade mentioned in the Hadith is the shade of God. This mistranslation is due to the misguided group Wahhabis and others that have infiltrated invalid creed and whoever believes in their ideology becomes a blasphemer like them. Their non-Islamic doctrine is a belief of Tajseem – which means likening Allah to the physical bodies, that explicitly belies the Qur'an and Sunnah.*

Prophet Muhammad, peace be upon him said, **"There are seven to whom Allah will grant shade on the day when there is no shade except this shade." The shade mentioned in this Hadith is the shade of the Throne – the Ceiling of Paradise.**

1. **"The just ruler.** Despite being in a position of power over people, he controls himself and is just with the other.

2. **The one who grows up adhering to the obedience of God** and stays away from sinning even when young.

3. **A man whose heart is attached to the mosque.** It is hard for the person to overcome evil inclinations and return to the mosque for every prayer. The one who overcomes his weaknesses and loves to come to the mosque for every prayer reaches a high status.

4. **The people who love each other for the sake of God.** They advise each other to do good deeds and to leave the evil deeds. They come together for the sake of God and leave each other for the sake of God.

5. **The person who resists the advances of a high-status and beautiful woman** who solicits them for immoral sexual behavior by stating, "I fear God. I do not engage in such actions."

6. **The person who gives generously to charity without seeking recognition or praise,** to the point where even their left-hand does not know what their right hand has given.

7. **The person who remembers and invokes the name of God when they are alone and is moved to tears** by their reverence and fear of their Lord.

When the Prophets and martyrs see this group of seven, they will be delighted for them due to their special status and the endowments they will receive on Judgment Day.

<<They slept very little during the night, busy in worship. And in the wee hours of the night, they were repenting. And concerning their monies, they dedicated a portion to the

needy and the deprived.>>

These righteous Muslims lived this way until Allah created their death.

What Happens to Sinner Muslims under the Sun?

People say, *"Is there anyone who can intercede for you?"*

The people will say to each other: *'Go to Adam'.*

They go to Adam and say, *"You are the father of humanity. Allah created you with a special status and commanded the angel to blow the noble soul into you. And God commanded the angels to prostrate themselves before you, Intercede for us with your Lord. Can't you see our suffering? Can't you see what happened to us?"*

> **Adam tells them, "Surely my Lord has unleashed a torture today such he has never unleashed before, nor will he ever unleash. He once forbade me to eat from the tree, and I disobeyed him. It's not me for this intercession. Go to someone else. Go to Noah, your father, after your father."**

And the people come to Noah and say, *"O Noah, you are the first of the Messengers sent to the peoples of the earth after they committed blasphemy. And Allah referred to you as His grateful servant. Intercede for us with your Lord. Can't you see what is happening to us? Don't you see we are suffering?"*

Noah answers them, "I had a plea answered, and I used it against my people. I am not the one for this intercession. Go to someone else, go to Abraham."

And so they go to Abraham, *"O Abraham, you are the Prophet of God. You are the one who is most devoted to your worship. (But that means after Muhammad) Intercede for us, by your Lord, don't you see we are suffering? Can't you see the suffering that has happened to us?"*

Abraham declares, "It is not me who defends this plea. Go to someone else. Go to Moses."

"O Moses, you are the Messenger of Allah. And Allah has chosen you for his message and Spoke to you among all people <besides Prophet Mohammed>. Intercede for us with your Lord. Can't you see what worries us? Can't you see the suffering that has happened to us?"

Moses replies, "I remember killing someone without being told to. It's not me for this intercession. Go to someone else. Go to Jesus."

And so, they go to Jesus and say, *"O Jesus, you are the Messenger of Allah, and you are the good news delivered to your mother Mary. You are that noble soul. You spoke to the people as a baby in the cradle. Intercede for us through your Lord. Don't you see we are suffering?"*

> **Jesus answers them, "I am not the one asking for this intercession. Go to someone else. Go to Muhammad."**

And so, they go to Muhammad, peace be upon him and say, *"O Muhammad, you are the Messenger of Allah, and you are the Seal of the Prophets. You are forgiven of sins and granted clearance from ever committing any sins your entire blessed life. "Intercede for us with your Lord."*

> **And the Prophet, peace be upon him, says, "I am the one for this. I am the one for this."** He will go under the throne and fall to his knees. Allah inspires Prophet Muhammad, peace be upon him, to praise Allah with praises that no one has ever praised God.
>
> He will be told, **"O Muhammad, lift your head and ask for what you wish and you will be granted. Intercede, and your intercession will be answered."**

He will lift his head and pray to Allah for the Muslims' relief. Because of his intercession, God saves a vast number of Muslim sinners from the agony of the sun.

As for the Blasphemers, they will say, ***"O my Lord, deliver me from the torment of the sun, even if it is by putting me into hellfire."*** *But they do not know the torture of the sun, and all the torments of Judgment Day are Minor compared to the Major torture of Hellfire, the Greatest Torture.*

Chapter 13
Hellfire ~ Vivid Description in the Qur'an
Tafsir in English

Prophet Muhammad, peace be upon him, said, **"Hellfire was ignited and fueled burning for one thousand years until it became red. And another thousand years until it became white. And then another thousand years until it turned black. And now the fire of Hell is pitch black."**

HELLFIRE, ALREADY IN EXISTENCE, was created to house all the accountable blasphemers who will reside in Hellfire forever without dying or their torture decreasing. There is also a place of Hellfire with unbearable cold. Giant scorpions the size of donkeys are there to torture their inhabitants. They drink boiling water and pus and eat things that will torture them forever.

The Prophet, peace be upon him, said, **"Allah enabled Hellfire to speak, and Hellfire complained and said, 'O my Lord, part of me has devoured the other part.' So, Allah created for Hell a cold section called 'Zamhareer'; it is so**

cold there that it also burns. God gave Hell a cold section and allowed Hellfire to take two breaths yearly. On that day, <God> will bring forth a portion of Hellfire."

These two breaths impact the Earth's temperature. One breath each year in the Summer causes the hottest day for the Earth that year, and one breath each year in the winter causes the coldest day for the Earth that year.

Although Hellfire does not have a soul, God has the Power to enable what He wills to speak and has the Power to create recognition in soul-less creations.

In Hellfire, the blasphemers will mock the Muslims that enter Hellfire by saying, *"Look, your faith did not benefit you because you're here too."*

Then, the Muslims will be taken out of Hellfire, leaving only the blasphemers in their misery. On the Day of Judgment, the <useless> idols worshiped by people in this life will be thrown into Hell.

The dwellers of Hell will be told, **"Had these idols been gods as you claimed, they would not have <joined you> and entered Hellfire."**

As for Paradise will not be full of all the human beings who enter it, so God will create beautiful creatures to inhabit the extra plentiful room in Paradise.

God Revealed the following Quran verses that mean:

<<By God, you will certainly see Hell pulled by 70,000 reigns. Each reign is pulled by 70,000 angels (over a billion angels), pulling forth only a small portion of Hellfire. On that day, Hellfire will be brought along. On that day, the human will remember everything he did, but to no avail will your memory benefit you on that day.>>

Upon seeing a portion of Hellfire, the disbelievers will be horrified.

<<The blasphemers say, "Woe is me. If only I had prepared for my afterlife. They will see it from the molten that's the station of Judgment Day, where they are on the reformed Earth. They will see that Hellfire brought forth to them. They will be taken towards the Hell.>>

<<Onward. March towards that which you used to deny. Go towards the Hell; that Hell that comes out of it is a huge column of smoke. That column of smoke that comes out of Hell is so big that it separates into three different columns. It is of no use against the flame. It shall not protect you or give you any relief. Surely, Hellfire throws out sparks as huge as castles, as if they are thick ropes of ships twisted together.>>

<<Whoa on that day, to the be-liars. There shall be a bridge on Judgment Day. One end of that bridge is on the reformed Earth, and the other will be at land outside the gates of

Paradise. Paradise is not level with the Earth; instead, it is much higher. That bridge is wide and slippery, traveling upward in the direction of Paradise, and beneath the bridge is Hellfire.>>

<<Everyone shall come to Hell <meaning> everyone shall come to the bridge over Hell.>>

Some people will enter Hellfire while other people will pass by safely. This bridge is one of Judgment Day's scariest, most dangerous stages. As for the Blasphemers (disbelievers), they all will fall off the bridge from their first step into the depths of Hell. It takes 70 years of falling into it to reach the bottom. But the sinner Muslim who enters Hell will not get to the bottom, and their torture is much less than that of the non-Muslims. Any suffering in Hellfire is unbearable, and no one can tolerate it.

<<When cast in, thrown therein, they hear a terrible roar like a donkey's bray. Its sound is powerfully deafening, and its flames are boiling as if it will explode. The disbelievers will be driven towards Hell in groups until they reach a place where they must wait until the gates of Hell open. And while they are waiting, more people are coming behind them until its gates open.>>

<<And the keepers of Hell are the angels who scold them (disbelievers) by saying, "Did there not come to you, messengers from amongst yourselves? Didn't there come to you Messengers reciting upon you the verses of your Lord and warning you about this day of yours?" They say, "Indeed."

But the Eternal Decree to torture the disbelievers has been fulfilled. "Our fates have come to be, and destiny has come upon us. Indeed, they did come to us, Warners, but we belied them. And we said, 'Allah never revealed anything.' And we said to those Messengers, "You are not in anything but a big misguidance." You are lost.>>

> **<<And they say, "Had only we listened, and had only we used our (sound) minds, then we would not have been among the inmates of the Inferno." They confess their wrongdoing of Blasphemy, but damned are the inmates of Hell. Their confession shall avail them not.>>**

<<It is said, 'Enter through the gates of Hell forever and ever abiding therein. And what a bad abode is that one for the arrogant one?' It has seven gates, and there is a section for every gate. And this Hell, it is its specific realm. It has an independent land with its ceiling and walls. The entire Earth and more can fit inside of Hell.>>

<<And every time a batch of people are thrown into Hell or fall into Hell, Hellfire itself will be asked, "Are you full? And it will say, "Is there more?" And then it will keep receiving batches and batches of people until it says, "I'm full. Enough, enough." And so those batches of people, they enter Hell wave after wave. And the people who were in Hell before hate the new group that came into Hell after them.>>

<<It will be said to the dwellers of Hell, 'This is a wave of newcomers into Hell crowding with you. And so, they say, 'No welcome to them. They are nothing but burned ones of the fire.' And so, the newcomers respond by saying, "Rather no welcome to you. You are the ones who offered this place to us by calling us to Blasphemy. Indeed, we were your followers. So, can you ward off any of the torture of Hell?" Those arrogant leaders will say, "We are all in this together." Certainly, Allah has finalized the judgment between the slaves.>>

<<Those newcomers say, "Our Lord, whoever offered this place to us then increased him a double torture in Hell." And those blasphemers in Hell will be looking for Muslims, and they say, "What's wrong with us? We don't see here now with us some people that we used to think were among the worst. Are they in Paradise, and we have wrongfully taken them as jokes? Or are they here with us, but our eyes have missed them?>>

<<Surely what has been described is indeed true and inevitable. It shall happen. What is it? The disputing of the people of Hell. When all the people of Hell are finally inside, the reformed Earth, Sun, and Moon will all be thrown into Hellfire. They will increase the fuel, making the flames even more powerful. The fuel of this <everlasting> fire is people and stones.>>

<<Then Hellfire shall be sealed from all its openings, and they will be surrounded <by flames> from every direction.

Then, the bars that lock those doors will come down, and the fire shall bounce back onto them. And once the dwellers are there, they live there and experience the torture therein. And on that day, no one shall torture as Allah tortures, and no one shackles as Allah shackles. They shall be in Hell, like pushing through the mud, struggling to go forward. And they will be burned by a scorching fire.>>

The shackles of the people of Hell are nothing like what has been witnessed on Earth as they go inside their bodies and come back out. Allah will increase their size because if not for that massive size, their bodies would disintegrate instantly in Hellfire. Allah will make them so large physically that the distance between one person's shoulders is the distance of three days of walking. His tooth, or molar, will be as big as Mount Uhud (7 km wide), gigantic, and his skin 40-60 cubits thick (60-90ft of skin), very huge. Their skins will burn away and melt, producing liquid pus.

<<Whenever their skins finish cooking, Allah recreates for them new skin so they can taste the torture <forever>. Indeed, Allah has always been (eternity) undefeated and wise. And this pus that's among the things that the people of Hell consume because they're starving, they're in there starving and can't even help themselves. >>

<<Is the pleasure of Paradise better? Or the Tree of Zaqqoum. What's the Tree of *Zaqqoum*? Indeed, it is a tree that exits from the base of Hell. Its pollen has the shape of the devil's head. Wherever they are in Hell, they come to

it, eat from it, and fill their bellies with it. Then, they follow their eating by drinking a concoction with scolding hot water. Then they eventually go back to wherever they came from in Hellfire.>>

<<They found their forefathers misguided, and they strongly and proudly strove in their legacy, the legacy of their forefathers. When they drink what they drink, it cuts right through their intestines and comes out from the bottom. They are given a drink from springs whose water is at the extremity of boiling, as hot as hot water could be. They eat from a stinking plant called Dareeˆ, whose flavor is horribly bitter. It doesn't make them fat, and it does not relieve their hunger.>>

<<Those who blasphemed will have cut for them clothing made from fire and poured over their heads, scolding water like acid that melts their insides and skins. For them, there are whips made of iron. And those who stored away the gold and the silver, and did not spend it for the sake of Allah <they didn't pay their Zakat>. Then, give them the news of a painful torture. On that day, when that gold and silver shall be heated in Hellfire, their foreheads will be branded by it and their sides and backs. This <punishment> is what you have stored away and made a treasure for yourselves.>>

<<So, taste the torture from your treasure. Every time the dwellers want to get out of the flames and out of the gloom, when they try to climb out of Hell, they find an angel at the top who smacks them back down, so they return to it. And it

said, "Taste the torture of the burning." And on that day, the idols the people worshiped will be in Hellfire with them, and the heat will come out of them. And who will be at the very, very bottom of Hell?>>

<<Those who used to show <outwardly> that they were Muslims while they knew that they were not Muslims <*Munafiq – a Muslim Pretender, a non-believer who hides his Blasphemy in his heart*>. After they are in Hell for a long time and see that some Muslims are still in Hell with them, they will mock the Muslims by saying, **"Look at you, you're still here. What has your religion done for you?"** Upon saying this mockery, Allah will remove the last Muslims out of Hellfire, and upon witnessing this, the blasphemers will be filled with misery, knowing they will stay in Hell forever and ever without death.>>

<<They call out to the keeper of Hell and Master Angel, "Malik, let your Lord make us die. Ask your Lord to make us die." They're begging him and repeatedly asking him and begging him. After 1000 years later, Angel Malik replies to them, "Surely you are here to stay." And those in Hell say to the keepers of Hell, "Call upon your Lord for us. Make du^ah for us. Ask Allah so that he would lighten some of the torture for us, just for a day?" >>

<<Those angels say, 'Did there not come to you Messengers assigned to you who gave you evidence?' They say, "Indeed." So, the angels say, "Then you make Du^ah." The supplication of the disbelievers in Hell is futile. They will be in Hell for a

time (Ages forever). When one Age ends, (instantly) a new age begins with a new torture. And they spend that time in that torture in Hell until that Age is over. Then, a new era instantly begins with a different torture, which continues until another period starts with a different unbearable torture, continuing like this forever. When they are in Hell, they shall never taste anything cool and have nothing to drink except for the scalding water and the boiling pus. A fitting payment for their Blasphemy.>>

They will dwell there for endless ages without any relief, not even a second—Yallatif, O God, Most Merciful. Protect us and have mercy on us from this tremendously wicked place. There is no relief from torture in Hellfire, not even for a second, forever and ever and ever.

Why do the blasphemers end up like this?

Blasphemers neglected their most essential obligation to worship God validly, which requires valid Islamic Knowledge and adherence and not learning from random fake and unqualified people online. Many inmates of the inferno were atheists in this life, and many followed man-made invalid religions that worshipped other than Allah.

Those who worshipped Satan, or Prophet Jesus and Lady Maryam, or Ezra or imagined God to be a body sitting on the throne or that He comes down at night; and even some past or present leaders who falsely claimed Godhood, they are all Pagan worshippers deserving of Hellfire because no creation is God.

Chapter 14

Paradise ~ Vividly Described in the Qur'an

Tasir in English

Paradise is above the seventh sky (Heaven) and not connected to it. The Grand Throne, also known as *Al-^Arsh, is its ceiling but exceeds* Paradise in vastness and size. Paradise is the confirmed blissful abode that God has already created for Muslim believers. God created this blessed place to remain everlastingly intact and unspoiled.

Prophet Adam first lived in Paradise for 130 years before spending the rest of his 1000-year life on Earth for 870 years. Therefore, historically, Paradise is confirmed to have existed for a long time.

Paradise has 100 levels, and the distance between each grade is like the distance between the Earth and the first sky (approximately 500 years distance). The highest level is called **'Al-Firdaws.'** Although many other rivers exist in Paradise, God created four special rivers of water, milk, honey, and non-intoxicating wine sourced from Al-Firdaws.

God described some aspects of Paradise in **Surat-ul Ghashiyah** by revealing that <<It has running water that does not become contaminated and spoils like the water on Earth.

Paradise has many places to sit, made of gold and various jewels, like rubies and emeralds. These seats remain elevated high up unless the people of Paradise want to sit on them. At which time, the cushion descends for the person to sit and then flies high up so that its occupants will see the spectacular views and wonders of Paradise.>>

The People of Paradise praise God as effortlessly as breathing in this life. Paradise is always bright because there's no night or darkness, but God creates a sign to show when a day has passed without sunrise or sunset.

The People of Paradise have the physical form of their forefather, Adam. They will all be 60 cubits tall and seven cubits wide, with attractive bodies free of bothersome body hair. Their head of hair, eyebrows, and eyelashes will be beautiful, and the men will be without beards.

Paradise has no filth: *no mucus to spit, no nose blowing, no urinating or defecating, no menstruation for women, and no childbirth. All the enjoyments of this Earthly life compared to the pleasures of Paradise are like a trace of water from a dipped needle compared to the vast ocean water.*

The Following Are Verses from the Holy Qur'an About Paradise:

<<They see Paradise getting closer and closer and closer. Paradise will be vast, much wider than Hell by thousands of times. It has eight gates and a ceiling, which is the ˆArsh

(Grand Throne), the largest creation. Crossing the bridge ensures safety. Next, the believers will head to the Basin (Al-HawD), sometimes referred to as a lake, and the HawD of our Prophet, peace be upon him, is the most massive. This body of water is whiter than snow and milk, sweeter than honey and sugar, and more fragrant than musk.>>

The water comes from the Kawthar River in Paradise and flows through a pipe into the basin. The Basin of Prophet Muhammad, peace be upon him, is as comprehensive and long as a sea, spanning a month in both directions because of its vastness. Prophet Muhammad's Basin is the largest among all the prophets' basins.

The cups surrounding it are like the stars in the sky in their abundance, representing the vast number of followers of Prophet Muhammad, peace be upon him. Drinking from this basin will provide believers everlasting relief from thirst and hunger. Once they enter Paradise, they will eat and drink solely for pleasure.

<<Enter Paradise in safety. That is the day of everlastingness. They have all they wish inside, but Allah has even more. The first one to enter Paradise is Prophet Muhammad, peace be upon him. He will take hold of the ring on the door of Paradise and move the ring. The angel will open the door and say, ***"You are the one for whom I was ordered to open the door, and no one shall enter it before you."***>>

<<Those who come to Paradise are those who feared their Lord. They will be driven towards the Garden in groups until they arrive, and its doors will be already open. And the keepers of Paradise, the angels, say to the believers entering, ***"Peace be upon you. You have done well. Congratulations! Enter Paradise Forever, enter Paradise for what you used to do."***>>

The believers are entering Paradise in groups and at intervals. A vast number of believers are entering the gates of Paradise. Prophet Muhammad's Nation will be the first nation to enter Paradise, where each entrance is as wide as a month.

The first group of 70,000 followers of Prophet Muhammad will enter Paradise with no judgment, questions, or punishment and have shining faces like the sun or a full moon. Each thousand will bring 70,000 individuals to enter Paradise without judgment or torture. The total count of individuals in this group is 4.9 billion.

This number is only part of the people of this Muhammadan Nation who will enter Paradise. The second group will be 70,000 Muslims with faces shining like stars who praise God.

In Paradise, two-thirds of the inhabitants will come from the nation of Prophet Muhammad, and the other one-third will be Muslims from all previous nations from Prophet Adam until Prophet Jesus, peace be upon them.

During the miracle Night Journey and Ascension of Prophet Muhammad, peace be upon him; the Prophet said, **"I entered Paradise and saw that most of its inhabitants were the poor."** Most of the Dwellers of Paradise will be those Muslims who were poor on Earth and will enter Paradise 500 years before the rich Muslims. The reason for this is that the acquisition of wealth demands greater scrutiny of its origins.

<<They are the trailblazers, the forerunners in doing good deeds and entering Paradise. They are especially elite ones, basking in gardens of bliss.>> *Who are they? They are a group that originated from the start of this nation, the nation of Muhammad, peace be upon him. The first group to follow Muhammad was larger, whereas fewer people from his nation followed in later generations.*

<<And the People of the Right. What a status the People of the Right have! The people who received their books in their right hands are basking in smooth, thornless Sidr (Jujube) trees and banana trees so loaded that their trunks are invisible. They will enjoy extended shade and water flowing over the surface without banks and abundant fruits.>>

<<The people of the right always have access to those fruits on elevated mattresses, which never go out of season. They are a group from the beginning of this nation and a group from the end of this nation.>> *The description pertains to the second level, not the first and best ones.*

<<And if <the believer's> good and bad deeds are equal, then he will have to stand near the wall and wait while others <who are higher rank> enter Paradise first.>> *Some scholars believe the Wall of Al-A∧raaf is the Wall of Paradise. Other scholars believe it is a wall God will create on Judgment Day near Paradise.*

<<There will be a barrier to separate the party of the believers from the party of the disbelievers. Men at the wall of Al-Aˆraaf can distinguish between believers and disbelievers by their sign. The radiance of their faces is a sign to recognize the believer, and the darkness of their faces and eyes is a sign to recognize the blasphemer.>>

<<Those on the wall call out to the People of Paradise, greeting **"Salaamun ˆaleykum."** They are yet to enter Paradise, and their hope remains intact. And when their eyes look towards the fire inmates, they will say, ***"O our Lord, do not put us with the unjust people."***>>

<<The People of the Wall (Al-Aˆraaf) identify men by their sign and call out to them. They will say to those that they recognize from their sign as blasphemers, "Your accumulation of money and your arrogance was of no avail to you.">>

<<Did those who entered Paradise include those whom you swore Allah would never give His mercy to in this world? Those people are in Paradise, and you're in Hell.>>

<<Those at the wall will be told, **"Enter Paradise without fear or sadness."** If you were to see that place, you would see a magnificent realm full of pure bliss.>>

The highest level of Paradise is Firdawss, which is Paradise. What most are calling Heaven *Al-Jannah* means *'The Garden'*, and it's called Al-Jannah because it is full of gardens.

<<For whoever feared God's punishment on Judgment Day, <meaning, i.e., the Muslim who followed the Islamic rules, performed his obligations, and avoided the unlawful in this worldly life> he will have two special gardens in Paradise. Paradise has a garden filled with everything golden and another with everything silver. The gardens are home to an abundance of leafy branches that bear plenty of fruit. Two springs flow in those gardens.>>

<<Aside from the two special gardens, there are two additional ones. The greenery is so intense that it appears black. In the center of the Garden, two erupting springs are in a special location. Paradise or Firdawss is the name given to the highest point of the Garden. Directly above Firdawss is the Grand Throne (the ceiling of Paradise) with chandeliers. All the rivers of Paradise originate from Al-Firdawss and flow throughout Paradise.>>

<<This Garden has rivers of fresh, delicious water that never goes stale, rivers of milk whose flavor never changes, rivers of <non-intoxicating> wine that is delicious and does not intoxicate or cause headaches, and rivers of pure honey that are not animal sources. <The milk is not from cows, and the

honey is not from bees>. Paradise contains rivers beyond the ones mentioned. The stones of Paradise are precious stones and pearls forming a majestic and gloriously beautiful kingdom.>>

<<A luxuriously happy place that is vast, full of brilliant shining light, fragrant musk, stable elevated castles, continually flowing rivers, lots of ripe fruits, beautiful wives, and many endowments in an everlasting abode. In Paradise, only pure animals exist, like winged horses with ruby-like bodies and wings made of gold. There are things we know and are yet to discover in Paradise. The swaying of the trees of Paradise in the breeze produces a sound that's more beautiful than music.>>

> The Messenger of Allah, peace be upon him, said, **"Surely in Paradise, there is a gigantic tree. This tree's shade is so expansive that a horse rider can ride for 100 years and remain under it. Designer beautiful clothing grows ready-made on a tree called Toubah in Paradise."** *Eliminating the need for work to design, cut, or sew.*

The inhabitants of Paradise will love the beautiful sound it produces when the trees sway, which is more pleasing than music.

> **<<Upon entering, the angels will proclaim to the People of Paradise, "Surely you are granted health and will never become ill. You are granted immortal life and will never die. You are granted everlasting youth, and you will never grow old. You have been granted luxury and will never be unhappy.">>**

<<Surely this is a reward for you. Your endeavor of worshiping on Earth is accepted and recognized. And then he will be in acceptable living. Lounging on green cushions, and there are pillows there that are lined up and carpets that are spread all around. They are lounging on mattresses filled with **stedrock** - a type of silk. So those mattresses are so soft, comfortable, and luxurious. In a garden high in place and high in prestige.>>

<<And upon them shall be delicate green silk garments called **'Sundus.'** And they will have thick silk and be adorned in silver bracelets, and their Lord shall give them a pure drink. They will drink a cup mixed with ginger from a special spring called **'Sal-Sabeel.'** In Paradise, some furniture is very high in the air. If the believer wants to sit on it, it just comes down for him, bending down like a camel bends down. Then he will sit upon it like royalty who sits upon a throne, and it raises him high to be able to look down and enjoy the view of Paradise.>>

<<They don't see any sun in there, they don't experience any bitter cold, and there's no moon. Although Paradise is always bright, they have night <without darkness>. The dwellers

in Paradises will have a sign for night-time and a sign for daytime.>>

All people of Paradise will be at the age of 33 years, and no one is unmarried in Paradise. Even babies that die young will be 33 years old and married in Paradise. All the dwellers will have new everlasting bodies but have the same soul when they go to Paradise.

<<They never get exhausted in Paradise and are not put out.>>

All the bodies are similar to the stature of Adam, peace be upon him, who was about 90 feet tall and 10 feet across. The least beautiful person in Paradise will be as beautiful as Prophet Joseph was in this life.

<<They will not have hair on their bodies except the hair of their heads, eyebrows, and eyelashes so that none of their beauty is concealed. They don't have anything dripping from their noses, they don't urinate, and they don't defecate. They only sweat, which is a beautiful fragrance similar to musk. The people in Paradise will be there with their <Muslim> families.>>

<<And those who believed, and their children followed them in faith, then Allah will give their children a status like the status of the parents. And Allah will not deprive the parents of any of their rewards in any way. Every individual is responsible for their deeds.>>

<<And among the endowments are good, nice mannerly, pretty wives. In Paradise, they have nice manners. <If your wife gives you some lip here in the Dunia, God willing, she won't give you any lip in the afterlife in Paradise, and you'll be nice to her, too.> The occupants of the Garden will be busy with their spouses in the shade, lounging on couches.>>

<<And the shade of Paradise will come close over them, and the fruits will be there subject to their desire, and they enjoy sexual climax but without any disgusting fluids or annoying smells. The wives in Paradise don't menstruate, and they are there forever.>>

Who are Al-Hoor-Al-^een? The human males will be more numerous than the human females in Paradise. God created for human males, gorgeous non-human women in Paradise called **Al-Hoor-Al-^een. They are** not human descendants of Prophet Adam and never lived on Earth, yet they will be very suitable for human Muslim males. Their name means 'They have big, beautiful eyes with very black iris, and the whites of their eyes are very white.' God created these women to be given as wives to the human men destined for Paradise.

The human men of Paradise will have at least two of these wives, and some will have much more. The Hoor-Al-∧een women are so beautiful, pure, and delicate that their husbands can see through their translucent skin to the inside bones of their legs.

None of the Dwellers of Paradise dispute or hate each other because their hearts are all like one heart, loving each other.

Some men will have more than two wives, and the women will have one husband and be very happy.

<<And the women of Paradise who are called Al-Hoor-Alˆeen, they will be wives for the men of Paradise, wives who only have eyes for their husbands. They are females of Paradise, not humans or genies, and no human before them or genie has ever touched them. They are very, very beautiful. The black of their eyes is very black, and the white of their eyes is very white, and they have stunning wide eyes.>>

<<As beautiful as concealed pearls with veiled faces that are intense and so pure you can see their bones through them (like translucent skin like pearl). And the Al-Hoor-Al-ˆeen, God created them without them being born, and God made them virgins, beloved to their husbands and similar in age, and every time the man is finished being with his wife, then Allah will restore her virginity.>>

If a married couple were both Muslims and died as Muslims, then in the afterlife, they would be married in Paradise. The human Muslim woman who lived on this Earth with all its struggles will have a much higher status in Paradise than Al-Hoor-Al-ˆeen. The human wife in Paradise will not be jealous of her husband's other wives. Everyone will be happy, delighted, satisfied, and enjoying whatever their heart desires. They will not have children, and nor will they wish to have children. They will never feel tired, poor, or sad. Married couples have sexual intercourse in Paradise.

<<And in Paradise, there are homes made of one gigantic, hollowed pearl, 60 miles high by 60 miles wide. The castles and palaces of Paradise are made from gold and silver bricks - alternating a golden brick and a silver brick, and the mortar for these brinks has a beautifully strong musk fragrance. Some people in Paradise will have very high chambers, and other people in Paradise will point to their high chambers as we point to the stars of the Earth's sky.>>

<<Also, there are palaces in Paradise where you can see the inside from the outside. In Paradise, they talk to each other, gathering, meeting, and visiting each other. Between them are their servants surrounding them.>>

Who are those servants? Immortal Youths are dwellers of Paradise who are young boys who never grow up. Some Muslim scholars said those are the children of the blasphemers in this life who died before puberty. But other scholars said, 'They are not human.' Each person in Paradise will have many delightful servants. At the least, a person in Paradise will have 10,000 servants serving him while carrying trays of gold and silver. These servants are non-human youths who have never lived on Earth. They are lovely, like untouched pearls.

The women of Paradise wear something that covers their heads without hiding the beauty of their hair. If a portion of this material came to this Earth or part of this woman's finger appeared in this life, the whole Earth would illuminate. The hair-combs are made of gold in Paradise. The incense burners contain Al-ˆOud, the most expensive fragrance on Earth. The Al-ˆOud of Paradise does not need fire to release a scent. The sweat of the people of Paradise is musk. Instead of urine and defecation, this beautiful fragrance comes from the perspiration of the pure believers' after eating and drinking.

<<If you were to see them, you would consider them scattered pearls, serving cups, and pitchers – a big container with the drink, and goblets are cups without handles. The goblets are silver, as pure as glass, and the glass is made from silver. Goblets of wine flow from springs, and there are pillows to lean comfortably against. The finest carpets are spread across for the delight of the believers. They do not experience headaches from it, and it never runs out. And (a wide array) of fruits of all sorts that they choose from.>>

<<Some of those fruits that they eat are familiar to them. Whenever they are provided with the fruits therein, they say, "This is what we recognize from the Dunia." <But it's not the same exactly. It's just Paradise's version of that fruit. And the pleasure in it being recognizable is that the human being enjoys what is recognizable.> And as soon as they pluck a fruit, a new one grows in its place immediately. And the flesh of birds that they desire is seen flying. If he desires to eat it, the bird will fall for him, and by the time it reaches him, it's cooked <broiled> and ready to eat. Then he eats it for enjoyment, and when done, <God> recreates the bird, and it flies away.>>

<<They hear nothing trivial, fruitless talk, or absurdities in Paradise. What they hear is "Salaam, Salaam." They approach each other, asking, "Surely, in the previous life, we were compassionate to our families. And so, Allah endowed upon us, saving us from the scorching wind's torture. Surely, in the worldly life, we used to call upon Allah, we used to make Du∧ah, and we used to pray to him and ask him." Surely, Allah is the one who was good to his slaves, and He is the one who was merciful to the believers.>>

The people of Paradise love each other and have no problems with each other. A man in Paradise will have more than one wife, but none of his wives would hate that or be jealous or bothered by that reality in any way. It doesn't bother them; they don't dislike each other, have evil thoughts, or have any inclination to sin.

<<Allah removes from their hearts what hatred they had in the earthly life. They will talk to each other while they recline on the luxurious furniture that flies them where they want to go. They approach each other, asking one another. One of them says, **"In the Dunia, i.e., the Earthly Life, I used to have a friend who was a disbeliever. He used to say to me, 'You're a Muslim?! Is it that after we die and then we turn into soil and bones, we will come back to life and be judged?!'**>>

<<So that Muslim in Paradise talking to the other Muslims, he says to them, **"Look!"** So, he looks, and he sees that Kafir, who was his friend amidst Hell. And he says to him, **"You almost ruined me. And had it not been for the endowment**

of my Lord, I would have been among those who are present in Hell. Now look at us here in Paradise. Shall we die here in Paradise? We shall not die here in Paradise; we already died and came back to life. And now we're in Paradise, and we're not getting tortured. Surely this is the great victory!!">>

<<And that blasphemer feels horrible when he hears that from that Muslim. The people in Hell hear the people in Paradise enjoying themselves. And the people of Hell call to the people of Paradise and say, "Pour upon us water or give us something that Allah has provided to you.">>

<<They say, "**Allah has made both of those forbidden for the blasphemers who took their religion as a joke, and they were enticed to prefer the earthly life. And so today, they shall be left in Hell to be tortured forever and ever, as if they are forgotten, just like they forgot about preparation for this day."**>>

The last Muslims will come out of Hell. They will be burnt, devastated, and destroyed when they leave Hell. Their bodies are charred like black coal, except for the parts that used to touch the ground when they prostrate in prayer. Those parts will not be affected by the fire. Their charred and burnt bodies will be submerged in the Basin, and Allah will revitalize them, restoring their health and beauty before being admitted into Paradise. The last believer who comes out of Hell will be burnt to a crisp, dipped into the HawD, revitalized, and placed at Paradise's entrance. When he looks in, he sees the believers enjoying themselves.

<<So, he says, **"O Allah, it's full."** Then he would be asked, **"Would you be satisfied with as much as the earthly life for yourself?" He would say, "Yes." He would be told, "You will have ten times that pleasure."**>>

The person with the lowest status in Paradise and the lowest Muslim rank has property that takes 1000 years to cross. It was reported that the last Muslim who gets out of Hellfire is named **'Juhayna.'**

<<For those who did good for them is what? **Al-Houssnah** - that's Paradise.>>

And something else, something extra. What is that extra? Because Paradise is already the best. So, what's more than that? What more can there be?

<<Seeing God without Him being in a place or direction.>>

The believers will stay in Paradise forever and ever.

<<They say, **"Al-Hamdulillah, Praise be to Allah, the One who fulfilled His promise to us and gave us this land and allowed us to go throughout Paradise wherever we wish."**

Oh, how good of a reward for those who practice their religion <only Authentic Islam is valid>.

And you'll see the angels circling the ^Arsh (Grand Throne) who glorify their Lord Allah, saying, ***"SubHan-Aallah and Al-Hamdulillah."***

And the judgment between them has been finalized in justice. And the believers are in Paradise saying, ***"Al-Hamdulilah Rabbil ˆAalameen,"*** which means ***"Praise be to Allah the Lord of the Universe"***>>

O Allah. We ask You to grant us entrance into Paradise and to receive the enjoyment of its pleasures forever!

O Allah. Protect us and our loved ones from any torture in the Hereafter!

O Allah. Guide us, our loved ones, and forgive our sins.

We ask You, O Allah, to accept our prayers. O God, by the virtuous status of our honorable Prophet Muhammad, the Prophet of mercy!

Praise and Gratitude to God, The Almighty and Lord of the Universe, the One and Only God, clear of having a son or any partner in Godhood.

Chapter 15

Qur'an Tafsir in English

About Resurrection

IF YOU ARE LIKE most people today, you are aware of the Law of Attraction that says, avoid negative thinking because they claim, 'You attract what you think.' However, that is not the whole truth. What God has predestined to happen will occur regardless of all your positive thinking.

Life on Earth is a Dream.
And the Afterlife is Reality!

Even if you never thought about dying, you will surely die. Just look at all the people worldwide who are dying suddenly. Even if you have never thought about these prophecies, they will happen, regardless of whether you are conscious of them or even believe in them.

Your belief in these events will not alter or affect what God has predestined to happen in the future at the prescribed time. Your thoughts won't affect the occurrence or timing of these events, whether you learn about them, obsess over them or completely avoid them.

You are living your life, and your choices are your permanent contributions to your Afterlife. A fake existence has no value.

If your life is full of lies and paradoxes, just like a novel or movie script, then your life is worthless. Prophetic events such as death and Judgment Day are inescapable, irrespective of your thoughts.

God revealed to humanity many Minor Signs that Judgment Day is near. As mentioned, all but one minor sign remains before the first of the Major signs begins.

The Major signs must undoubtedly happen before the world ends. The minor signs started happening for the last 1500 years, and what remains is the occurrence of one last minor sign to happen before the 10 Major signs begin.

None of the Major signs have started yet, but trustworthy, righteous Muslims expect the Major signs to begin within this decade, if not much sooner.

The world has worsened, and people must realize what happens after death. Ignoring this subject will cause you a devastating outcome. So stop pretending it is unimportant or you are courageous and utterly unphased by death. Your avoidance will not change the terrifying reality that awaits you in your grave.

I genuinely want the very best for you, which is to choose what is best. But only you must take action and actively make the right choice. Please read this series with an open heart, examine your life, and realize you have what it takes to be awake and conscious.

Regardless, most people prioritize comfort and convenience, even if it means losing Paradise. As you can see, giving up Paradise for temporary pleasure is illogical.

These pleasures are your adversaries, closing your eyes to the reality. If you stay comfortable all your life, nothing motivates you to examine and question your life so you can wake up from your deep slumber.

In this state, many individuals live with no drive to explore what is truly significant.

Do you have answers to the following?

- *Why are you alive and existing?*
- *What is your purpose on this earth?*
- *Why are you living in this century and not a previous or later century?*
- *What happens when we die? Will I be safe in the grave and beyond?*
- *Have you wondered why people are converting to Islam if you're not Muslim?*
- *Am I living a life that God accepts?*
- *Am I living my life as a knowledgeable, authentic, and*

real Muslim?

- *Am I performing good deeds ordained by God in compliance with valid religious knowledge?*
- *Does God even accept my good deeds?*
- *Which abode do I want to dwell in forever – Paradise or Hellfire?*
- *Am I living my life doing the actions of the people going to Paradise?*
- *Am I living my life doing the activities of the people going to Hellfire?*

Pain is a fantastic tool that cracks open your heart so you can finally witness reality and stop the fake and numbing dream.

Pain makes you question and motivates you to change.

Pain inspires you to ask questions to change your life or ways.

Pain is an excellent catalyst for self-awareness and consciousness rather than continuing with the status quo.

How do you expect to wake up to the reality of this temporary fleeting world?

What will wake you up from your deep mental sedation and robotic life? If you're obliviously unaware and your earthly life is a bed of roses, you'll feel you're in a fantastic, happy dream you never want to leave.

Unfortunately for you, this brief dream is all you'll ever have of pleasure—fleeting moments, and your entire life will be void of good deeds in the Afterlife. All of this happened because you were too occupied enjoying ONE pleasant dream. After death, you'll realize that you spent your entire life on what doesn't matter and you're spiritually bankrupt. From that moment onward, you will never experience pleasure forever and ever, which will be your ultimate tragedy.

So, what will wake you up before it's too late? Because if you don't wake up in time, your Afterlife will be the worst of miseries.

Every human soul here on earth will undoubtedly wake up; that's for sure! I mean everyone! The Angel of Death will wake all who is deeply unconscious with a sudden greeting of severe punishment and everlasting torture.

Losing the Afterlife is a serious matter. The most dreadful thing that can happen is to die without proper belief and awaken to the fleeting nature of this life upon death. If that becomes your reality, you have failed gravely in the Afterlife.

If you remain a disbeliever or a fake believer, only identifying as Muslim by name because of extreme ignorance, then this message is for you too. The number of fake Muslims in our world today is astonishing. Many people go through life smiling and laughing, only to be awakened abruptly by the greeting of the angel of death with God's everlasting punishment. If you identify with this, your Afterlife will be the worst tragedy.

Why? The Afterlife is everlasting, and so is your suffering.

All suffering on earth is temporary because this life is temporary. In contrast, losing the Afterlife is the worst catastrophe. It is far worse than losing everything valuable to you: from wealth, money, housing, possessions, and all you hold dear to your heart from family, children, and loved ones. **Compared to losing the Afterlife, losing everything in this world is minor.**

Ponder and contemplate both that and the information within this book. Please read all the books in the Sacred Veil Series to gain proper Islamic knowledge and prepare for the Afterlife. **Money doesn't buy you Paradise; Sincere Adherence to Authentic Islamic Knowledge does.**

The Following Verses in the Holy Qur'an are God's Warning to Humanity:

In Surat Hajj (22) Verses 5–12, God revealed these verses that mean:

<<O Humanity! If you are doubtful of Resurrection, then verily <Look at yourselves how you were created; then there is no reason to deny Resurrection except if you reject the obvious that> **God created you from soil and water** <This references Prophet Adam originated

from soil>, **then God created you from a sperm-drop <a mixture of male and female sexual fluid, i.e., the offsprings' of Adam>. Then God created you into a clot** <ˆAlaqah—which is thick coagulated blood>**, then into** <Mudghah> **a little lump of flesh** <the amount a person could chew>**—fully formed <those created with no impairment or disability> or undeveloped** <this includes: all people's appearance, height—shortness and tallness, their perfections, and imperfections;> **God changed you all from state to state, to demonstrate** <God's Power and Perfection to do what God Wills> **and make clear to you.**

This verse means that the Creator, with the Perfect Power and Will to create something from the soil, has the Power and Will to create anything to become a sperm drop. Nothing is difficult for Allah to create. There is no comparison between creating something from soil and water and creating a blood clot that becomes a Mudghah, then into bones. God is All-Powerful and has the Power to recreate all humans again as they were on the Day of Resurrection.

<Then> God created whom He willed, to remain in the wombs <embryo> for an appointed term <the delivery to full-term or miscarriage>**, then God create you as infants and gave you strength to grow into your prime age of adulthood. Among you, some** <may> **die** <young before becoming adults>**, while others may reach the feeblest stage of life so that they know nothing after having known much** *(or will no longer remember to benefit from knowledge as he cannot retain what he learns). <Allah gives another proof*

for Resurrection by saying> **And look at the earth that is barren-dead and lifeless, but as soon as God sends down rain on it, it begins to stir** <with growing life>, **and it swells, producing pairs of every type of pleasant plant.>> (22:5)**

ذَٰلِكَ بِأَنَّ ٱللَّهَ هُوَ
ٱلۡحَقُّ وَأَنَّهُۥ يُحۡيِ
ٱلۡمَوۡتَىٰ وَأَنَّهُۥ
عَلَىٰ كُلِّ شَيۡءٖ قَدِيرٞ ٦

<<That is because Allah <alone> **is the True God whose existence is a Must** <God's existence is a Mental Necessity—the Sound Mind will only accept that God must exist>. **God** <alone> **gives life to the dead** <as God revives the dead earth> **and God** <alone> **is the All-Powerful Creator Who creates what He Wills.>> (22:6)**

<<And certainly, the Final Hour <Judgment Day> **is coming. There is** <absolutely> **no doubt about it. And Allah never misses a deadline and will surely resurrect those** <all the humans> **in the graves.** <God promised Judgment Day and Resurrection; therefore, these events must come into existence>.>> **(22:7)**

وَمِنَ ٱلنَّاسِ مَن
يُجَٰدِلُ فِى ٱللَّهِ بِغَيْرِ
عِلْمٍ وَلَا هُدًى
وَلَا كِتَٰبٍ مُّنِيرٍ ٨

God revealed this Ayah about Abu Jahl <<**And among men is he** <meaning Abu Jahl> **who disputes about Allah's Attributes without** <knowing these three true sources> **Religious Knowledge, Evidence or Holy Scriptures.**>> **(22:8)**

ثَانِىَ عِطْفِهِۦ لِيُضِلَّ
عَن سَبِيلِ ٱللَّهِ ۖ لَهُۥ فِى
ٱلدُّنْيَا خِزْىٌ ۖ وَنُذِيقُهُۥ
يَوْمَ ٱلْقِيَٰمَةِ عَذَابَ
ٱلْحَرِيقِ ٩

<<<**Abu Jahl is> turning away** <in arrogance away from Islam and with no compassion for other people> **to lead** <others> **astray from Islam through his arguments** <Islam is the only religion accepted by God>. **For him <Abu Jahl will suffer in both worlds> there is disgrace for him in this worldly life** <by Abu Jahl being killed in the Battle of Badr>**, and on the Day of Resurrection, God will make him taste** <i.e. experience> **the torture of** <everlasting> **burning** <in Hellfire>.>> **(22:9)**

<<<Abu Jahl will be told and all disbelievers> **'This is <the compensation> for what your hands have done'** <of blasphemy, religious denial and lies>. *[God mentioned the hand because it is an instrument used for acquiring and*

getting] **And verily, Allah is never unjust to** <His> **slaves>> (22:10)**

<<And among humankind are those who worship Allah as if they were on the very edge <their faith is weak and not in the depth of their hearts> **If something good happens to them** <, i.e., good health or increase wealth>, **they will feel reassured, at peace and tranquil in the religion of Islam and in worshiping God. Still, suppose any trial or calamity struck them, i.e., in their health, illness in their body, or loss of their financial livelihood. In that case, they relapse**

[falling back into blasphemy—like a soldier waiting in anticipation to win to take his portion of the spoils. He will take any opportunity to escape and leave if he senses a loss. God revealed this verse during the time the Arabs made the migration to Medina. If one of them was in good health, his horse had a mare, his wife gave birth to a son, and his wealth and money were abundant, he would say, "I have experienced nothing but good since I became Muslim, and his heart would be content." If the opposite were to happen to him, he would say, "Ever since I became Muslim, nothing good has happened to me <that statement is blasphemy>."]

He loses both this world <When Abu Jahl was killed> **and the Hereafter** <by entering everlasting Hellfire>. <Losing both

worlds—this life and the Hereafter> **That is the obvious and most evident of losses.** [A loss no one can mistaken.]>> **(22:11)**

يَدْعُواْ مِن دُونِ ٱللَّهِ
مَا لَا يَضُرُّهُۥ
وَمَا لَا يَنفَعُهُۥۚ
ذَٰلِكَ هُوَ ٱلضَّلَٰلُ
ٱلْبَعِيدُ ١٢

<< (After committing apostasy) **They call upon their idols** <in worship> **that can neither harm him if he does not worship it nor benefit him by worshiping this idol** (since creations are not God). **That is** <their blasphemy> **truly the farthest misguidance that one can stray** <blasphemy is the farthest from the truth> >> **(22:12)**

إِنَّ ٱلدِّينَ عِندَ ٱللَّهِ
ٱلْإِسْلَٰمُۗ وَمَا ٱخْتَلَفَ
ٱلَّذِينَ أُوتُواْ ٱلْكِتَٰبَ إِلَّا
مِنۢ بَعْدِ مَا جَآءَهُمُ ٱلْعِلْمُ
بَغْيًۢا بَيْنَهُمْۗ وَمَن يَكْفُرْ
بِـَٔايَٰتِ ٱللَّهِ فَإِنَّ ٱللَّهَ
سَرِيعُ ٱلْحِسَابِ ١٩

God revealed in Surat Al-ˆImran verse 19, which means, <<**Certainly, the only religion Allah accepts is Islam. And those given the Scriptures** <from the Jews and Christians> **did not deviate from the truth** <leave Islam and the proper worship of God, by Tawheed—which means, knowing the difference between the Creator and all created things. However, the Christians invented a false ideology about God, claiming He is '3 in 1', and the Jews said, 'Ezra is the son of God.'>. **But their deviation originated from their conflict of mutual jealousy and envy** <because the deviators were pursuing Power, control, manipulation of the people, and financial profits.

Some Scholars said, ‘They differed about the Prophethood of Muhammad, peace be upon him. As some believed in him while others disbelieved.’ Other Scholars said, ‘The Christians differed amongst themselves about the Prophethood of Jesus when> **After the knowledge had come to them that Jesus is a Prophet and Messenger of God.’ And whoever disbelieves** (falls into apostasy) **and denies the Ayat,** i.e., Proofs, evidence, verses, signs, and revelations of Allah, **surely, Allah’s Reckoning** <whether that is compensation of reward or punishment> **is fast.>>**

Notice the difference between the correct interpretation of verses just mentioned by the Ancient Scholars and the following translation commonly found in the so-called Qur’an translations below.

God revealed in the **Holy Qur’an in Surat Al-ˆImran verse 19** that means, **<<Certainly, the only religion Allah accepts is Islam. And those given the Scriptures did not deviate from the truth but from their conflict of mutual jealousy and envy after the knowledge had come to them. And whoever disbelieves and denies the Ayat** <signs>. **Then surely, Allah’s Reckoning is fast.>>**

Beneficial Nightly Duˆah—Invocation:

The Muslim who recites **Verse 19 of Chapter Al-ˆImran** (the translation is above and the transliteration is as follows):

<<Innad-dina ^ind-Aallahil Islam wamakh-talafa-l-ladhina utul-kitaba illa mim-ba^di ma ja(4)' ahumul^ilmu baghyam baynahum, wa may-yakfor bi'ayat-illahi fa'inn-Allaha sari^ul Hisab.>>

And the Muslim who follows the verse by saying: **<<Wa ana ash-hadu bi maa Shahid-Allaah wa as-tawdi^u Allah hadhihi-shahadata wa hiya liy ^ind-Aallahi wadi^ah.>>**

This statement means, **"And I bear witness to what God witnessed, and I entrust God with this Shahadah** <Testifications of Faith>**—and it is my Trust for safekeeping with God."**

Prophet Muhammad, peace be upon him, said, **"The person who recites this Ayah at bedtime, Allah will create for him 70,000 creations that will supplicate to Allah to grant him forgiveness until Judgment Day."**

On Judgment Day, Allah will reveal what is translated to mean, **<<My servant has a covenant with me, and I am the worthiest of fulfilling the covenant—enter my servant into Paradise>>.** *Yaqulul-Allahi yawmal qiyyamah <<Inna li ^abdiy ^indiy ^ah-daa, wa ana aHaqqu man wafaa bil^ahd, ad-khilu ^abdiyal-Jannah>>.*

Call To ACTION

Thank you for your commitment to learning and for having the courage to read this book. My hope is that you are inspired to live with courage and integrity and have chosen to be among the conscious believers who prepare for Paradise, the everlasting abode of peace and bliss. It would mean a lot to me and other seekers of this information if you could take a moment to write a short review by sharing how you benefited and what was most memorable. Your kindness and support are greatly appreciated.

God Bless You!
Nada

Please scan QR Code to write a book review. Thank you in advance for writing a review!

Sacred Veil: Revealing Authentic Islam
Available in Paperback & eBook
[Hardcover & Audiobook Spring 2025]

The Final Hour Unveiled
Available in Paperback & eBook.
[Audiobook in Summer 2025]

www.ingramcontent.com/pod-product-compliance
Lightning Source LLC
LaVergne TN
LVHW050540160826
845677LV00011B/2105